Structured Exercises in

Management

Volume

3

Structured Exercises in

STRESS

Management

A Handbook for
Trainers, Educators, Group Leaders

Volume

3

Edited by
Nancy Loving Tubesing, EdD
Donald A Tubesing, MDiv, PhD

REPRODUCTION POLICY

Unless otherwise noted, your purchase of this volume entitles you to reproduce a modest quantity of the worksheets that appear in this book for your education/training activities. For this limited worksheet reproduction no special additional permission is needed. However the following statement, in total, must appear on all copies that you reproduce.

> Reproduced from *Structured Exercises in Stress Management, Volume 3*, Nancy Loving Tubesing and Donald A. Tubesing, Editors. © 1994 Whole Person Associates, 210 W Michigan, Duluth, MN 55802.

Specific prior written permission is required from the publisher for any reproduction of a complete or adapted exercise with trainer instructions, or large-scale reproduction of worksheets, or for inclusion of material in another publication. Licensing or royalty arrangement requests for this usage must be submitted in writing and approved prior to any such use.

For further information please write for our Permissions Guidelines and Standard Permissions Form. Permission requests must be submitted at least 30 days in advance of your scheduled printing or reproduction.

Library of Congress Cataloging in Publication Data

Structured exercises in stress management : A handbook for trainers, educators, and
  group leaders / Nancy Loving Tubesing and Donald A. Tubesing, eds.
  192p. 23cm.
    Summary: A collection of thirty-six exercises for stress management to be used
  by trainers and facilitators in group settings.
    ISBN 1-57025-016-2 (v.3 : pbk) : $29.95
      1. Stress (psychology)—Prevention, problems, exercises, etc. 2. Stress—
  Psychological, prevention & control, problems. I. Title. II. Tubesing, Nancy
  Loving III. Tubesing, Donald A.
  BF575.S75S74   1986, 1990, 1994
  158'.92—dc19   83-61073

Printed in the United States of America

10 9 8 7 6 5 4 3 2

Published by:

WHOLE PERSON ASSOCIATES
210 West Michigan
Duluth MN 55802
(800) 247-6789

PREFACE

Over a decade ago we launched an experiment in health education—the Whole Person series of **Structured Exercises in Stress Management** *and* **Structured Exercises in Wellness Promotion.** *We believed that it was time to move beyond peptalks and handouts to an experiential approach that actively involves the participant—as a whole person—in the learning process.*

What began as an experiment has become a catalyst for dramatic changes in health promotion and education! **Structured Exercises** *volumes have found their way into the libraries of trainers, consultants, group workers, and health professionals around the world. We're proud that these volumes have become classics—the resource of choice for planning stress management and wellness promotion programs.*

Our purpose in publishing this series was to foster inter-professional networking and to provide a framework though which we can all share our most effective ideas with each other. As you will soon discover, we scoured the country looking for the most innovative, effective teaching designs used by the most creative consultants and trainers in business, health care and social services, then included some of their most imaginative ideas in this volume.

Many of the exercises we designed ourselves and refined in hundreds of workshops we've conducted over the past twenty years. Some are new combinations of time-tested group process activities. Others were submitted by people like you who continually strive to add the creative touch to their teaching.

The layout of **Structured Exercises** *is designed for easy photocopying of worksheets, handouts and preparation notes. Please take advantage of our generous policy for reproduction—but also please be fair to the creative individuals who have so generously shared their ideas with you.*

☞ *You may duplicate worksheets and handouts for use in training or educational events—as long as you use the proper citation as indicated on the copyright page. Please also give written credit to the original contributor. Whenever we've been able to track down the source of an idea, we've noted it. Please do the same when you share these ideas with others.*

☞ *However, all materials in this volume are still protected by copyright. Prior written permission from Whole Person Press is required if you plan large scale reproduction or distribution of any portion of this book. If you wish to include any material or adaptation in another publication, you must have permission in writing before proceeding. Please send us your request and proposal at least thirty days in advance.*

*   **Structured Exercises** *are now available in two convenient formats. This small-format softcover version is produced with a new book binding process that stays open on your desk or podium for easy reference, and lies flat on the photocopier for quick duplication of worksheets.*

*   *Many trainers enjoy the wide margins and larger type of the full-size looseleaf format, which provides plenty of space for you to add your own workshop designs, examples, chalktalk notes, and process reminders for your presentations. The looseleaf version also includes a complete package of camera-ready worksheet masters for easy reproduction of professional-looking handouts.*

*   ☞ *See page 152 in the Resources section for complete descriptions and ordering information for worksheet masters and companion volumes of the* **Stress** *and* **Wellness** *series in softcover and looseleaf formats.*

*   *We are grateful to the many creative trainers who have so generously shared their "best" with you in this volume (see page 145) as well as others in the series. We hope that the ideas here stimulate your own creative juices.*

*   *So, go ahead. Strive to bring your teaching alive in new ways. Expand your stress management approach. Continue to touch and motivate people with learning experiences that engage and challenge them as whole persons.*

*   *Then let us know what works well for you. We'd love to consider your new ideas for inclusion in a future volume so that we can carry on the tradition of providing this international exchange of innovative teaching designs.*

Duluth MN   *Nancy Loving Tubesing*
January 1994   *Donald A Tubesing*

INTRODUCTION

Stress is a fact of life—and from the board room to the emergency room to the living room people are searching for ways to manage stress more positively.

Structured Exercises in Stress Management, Volume 3 offers you 36 designs you can use for helping people move beyond information to implementation. Each exercise is structured to creatively involve people in the learning process, whatever the setting and time constraints, whatever the sophistication of the audience. To aid you in the selection of appropriate exercises, they are grouped into six broad categories:

> *Icebreakers:* These short (10–20 minutes) and lively exercises are designed to introduce people to each other and to the subject of stress management. Try combining an icebreaker with an exercise from the assessment or management section for an instant evening program.

> *Stress Assessments:* These exercises explore the symptoms, sources and dynamics of stress. All the processes help people examine the impact of stress in their lives. You'll find a mixture of shorter assessments (30–60 minutes) and major theme developers (60–90 minutes). Any exercise can easily be contracted or expanded to fit your purpose.

> *Management Strategies:* Each of these processes explores the issue of overall strategies for dealing with the stress of life. Participants evaluate their strengths and weaknesses and identify skills for future development.

> *Skill Developers:* Each volume in this handbook series will focus on a few coping skills in more depth. The four exercises in this section highlight relaxation, surrender, laughter and interpersonal contact skills.

> *Action Planning/Closure:* These exercises help participants draw together their insights and determine the actions they wish to take on their own behalf. Some also suggest rituals that bring closure to the group process.

> *Energizers:* The energizers are designed to perk up the group whenever fatigue sets in. Sprinkle them throughout your program to illustrate skills or concepts. Try one for a change of pace—everyone's juices (including yours!) will be flowing again in 5–10 minutes.

The format is designed for easy use. You'll find that each exercise is described completely, including: goals, group size, time frame, materials needed, step-by-step process instructions, and variations.

☞ *Special instructions for the trainer and scripts to be read to the group are typed in italics.*

✔ Questions to ask the group are preceded by a check.

➤ Directions for group activities are indicated by an arrow.

● Mini-lecture notes are preceded by a bullet.

Although the processes are primarily described for large group (25 to 100 people) workshop settings, most of the exercises work just as well with small groups, and many are appropriate for individual therapy or personal reflection.

If you are teaching in the workshop or large group setting, we believe that the use of small discussion groups is the most potent learning structure available to you. We've found that groups of four persons each provide ample air time and a good variety of interaction. If possible, let groups meet together two or three different times during the learning experience before forming new groups.

These personal sharing groups allow people to make positive contact with each other and encourage them to personalize their experience in depth. On evaluations, some people will say "Drop this," others will say, "Give us more small group time," but most will report that the time you give them to share with each other becomes the heart of the workshop.

If you are working with an intact group of 12 people or less, you may want to keep the whole group together for process and discussion time rather than divide into the suggested four or six person groups.

Each trainer has personal strengths, biases, pet concepts and processes. We expect and encourage you to expand and modify what you find here to accommodate your style. Adjust the exercises as you see fit. Bring these designs to life for your participants by inserting your own content and examples into your teaching. Experiment!

And when you come up with something new, let us know . . .

CONTENTS

Preface v

Introduction vii

ICEBREAKERS

73 INTRODUCTIONS 6 1

In these two quick icebreakers, participants introduce themselves by describing someone who handles stress well and
explore their reactions to pressure. (10–20 minutes)

  A Models 1
  B Under Fire 2

74 AGENDA CONSENSUS 4

Participants use notecards to record their own expectations for
the meeting, then compare notes with others in the group and
identify which personal goals will and won't be met.
(15 minutes)

75 MARAUDERS 6

This highly active and entertaining sensory awareness exercise
demonstrates the physical symptoms of stress. Participants
learn to recognize their own unique patterns of reaction to
stress. (20–30 minutes)

76 PANDORA'S BOX 10

Participants get acquainted as they identify major sources of
stress and discover a surprise ending. (15–30 minutes)

77 TRAVELING TRIOS 12

In this fast-paced icebreaker participants move from group to
group, meeting with each other and describing their coping
styles. (10–15 minutes)

78 GOING TO JERUSALEM 14

Participants use stress symptoms to play an old-fashioned
icebreaker. (10–20 minutes)

STRESS ASSESSMENTS

79 SPICE OR ARSENIC? 17

Using an unusual measuring device, participants assess current
and past stress levels and decide how much is enough for
them. (20–30 minutes)

80 ON THE SPOT 21

In this thought-provoking process participants examine situations in which they are most vulnerable to manipulations, and
using **Ten Steps to Critical Thinking,** brainstorm ways to
avoid being manipulated in the future. (30–60 minutes)

81 DRAINERS AND ENERGIZERS 26

The checklists used in this exercise prompt participants to
identify the negative stressors in their lives that drain them, as
well as the positive energizers that refill them—at work, at
home and at play. (10–25 minutes)

82 LIFETRAP 3: SICK OF CHANGE 30

In this multi-phase exercise participants examine the role of
change in their lives and the stress it creates. The double
assessment, both objective and subjective, allows them ample
opportunity to explore their current risk level and to articulate
with each other the nature of the changes they are experiencing.
Finally, participants plan strategies for taking charge of their
own level and pace of change as they move into the future.
(60–90 minutes)

83 JOB DESCRIPTIONS 40

Participants divide into separate male and female groups to
examine how sex role stereotyping can lead to the interpersonal stress of conflicting expectations. (60 minutes)

84 THE LAST CHRISTMAS TREE 44

This fantasy exercise enables participants to explore the stress
associated with rejection. (20–30 minutes)

MANAGEMENT STRATEGIES

85 METAPHORS **49**

Participants study the form and function of various objects, seeking clues to creative stress management. (40–50 minutes)

86 S.O.S. FOR STRESS **54**

Participants learn an overarching paradigm for coping with stress and apply the specific strategies from this model to a personal stressor of their choice. (30–50 minutes)

87 STRESS CLUSTERS CLINIC **59**

In this thought-provoking card game participants utilize separate decks of stressor cards and coping cards to create stress scenarios and strategies for coping based on "the luck of the draw." (40–60 minutes)

88 CORPORATE PRESENTATION **66**

In this affirming small group activity, participants give themselves a lecture about the ten best methods for managing stress. (20–30 minutes)

89 IMAGINE SUCCESS **68**

Participants practice the technique of positive visualization, imaging themselves as successfully employing a selected coping skill. (15–30 minutes)

SKILL BUILDERS

90 CONFLICT MANAGEMENT **73**

In this thought-provoking learning experience participants explore four conflict-prevention skills and experiment with applying them to specific conflict situations. (60 minutes)

91 EIGHT-MINUTE STRESS BREAK **80**

Participants learn a 15-step stretch routine that can be used as a stress break any time of the day. (10 minutes)

92 STOP LOOK AND LISTEN **84**

Using a do-it-yourself study guide, trios of participants experiment with techniques to improve listening skills and explore applications of empathy as a stress management strategy. (60 minutes)

93 CENTERING MEDITATION **92**

Participants experience the quieting process of meditation and the focusing power of visualization in this guided fantasy. (25–40 minutes)

PLANNING & CLOSURE

94 CLOSING FORMATION **97**

In this round-robin ending participants pair up with many different partners to briefly share reactions, insights and coping plans. (10–30 minutes)

95 EXIT INTERVIEW **100**

In dyads participants review course content and publicly affirm their plans for improved stress management. (20–30 minutes)

96 RECIPE FOR SUCCESS WITH STRESS **104**

Participants reflect on the ingredients for successful stress management as they cook up innovative personal recipes for handling stress. (25–30 minutes)

97 MY STRESS REDUCTION PROGRAM **107**

This step-by-step planning process helps participants formulate a specific plan for managing a stress-related problem. (20–30 minutes)

98 CHANGE PENTAGON **110**

Participants explore each aspect of life (mental, physical, interpersonal, spiritual and lifestyle) seeking positive alternatives for managing stress. They then draw up a "whole person" plan for dealing with specific problem situations. (15–30 minutes)

GROUP ENERGIZERS

99 KICKING YOUR STRESS CAN-CAN 113

Participants kick up their heels as they symbolically kick sources of stress out of their lives. (5 minutes)

100 CHINESE SWING 114

In this invigorating exercise break participants learn an ancient oriental technique for releasing stress. (10 minutes)

101 CLOUDS TO SUNSHINE 116

This adaptation of a traditional T'ai chi exercise allows participants to breathe and stretch easily while imagining four different scenes from nature. (3–5 minutes)

102 CREATE A SINGALONG 118

Participants compose stress and coping lyrics for familiar melodies and then perform their "work" or the group. (10–15 minutes)

103 GROANS AND MOANS 120

In this noisy energizer participants experiment with an old-fashioned remedy for stress. (5–10 minutes)

104 TUG OF WAR 122

In this game of strategy, participants pair up to explore alternative approaches to conflict. (5–10 minutes)

105 WARM HANDS 124

In this brief introduction to the potential of autogenics, participants imagine their way to warm hands and a profound sense of relaxation. (5–10 minutes)

106 WHAT'S THE HURRY? 126

This touching parable points out how striving too hard to reach a goal may have stressful side effects. (5 minutes)

107 YOU'RE NOT LISTENING! 129

In this riotous energizer partners work hard at "not listening" to each other and then brainstorm essentials of good listening. (5–10 minutes)

108 PUSHING MY BUTTONS **131**

In this unusual self-care break participants stimulate several acupressure points to get their energy flowing again. (10–15 minutes)

RESOURCES

GUIDE TO THE RESOURCE SECTION **135**

TIPS FOR TRAINERS **136**

EDITOR'S CHOICE **138**
Four****Exercises: The Best of **Stress 3**
Especially for the Workplace

WINNING COMBINATIONS **141**
Generic Stress Presentation
Workshop on Stress with Skill-Building
    (Listening/Conflict)
Stress of Change Workshop

ANNOTATED INDEXES **143**
Index to Chalktalks
Index to Demonstrations
Index to Physical Energizers
Index to Mental Energizers
Index to Relaxation Routines

CONTRIBUTORS/EDITORS **148**

WHOLE PERSON PUBLICATIONS **153**

Icebreakers

73 INTRODUCTIONS 6

In these two quick icebreakers, participants introduce themselves by describing someone who handles stress well (**Models**) and explore their reactions to pressure (**Under Fire**).

GOALS

To get acquainted.

To raise consciousness about topics to be covered during the session.

GROUP SIZE

Unlimited; some modifications may be necessary with very large or very small groups.

TIME FRAME

10–20 minutes

MATERIALS

For **Under Fire:** matchbooks (one for every four participants); simple prizes (eg, raisins, gold stars, biodots) for the winning quartet.

PROCESS

Introduction A: MODELS

1) The trainer gives participants instructions for identifying a stress "model."

   ➤ Think about someone you know who handles stress well. This could be a co-worker, a friend, a family member, a public figure, even a TV character.

   ☞ *Pause until everyone has a stress model in mind.*

   ➤ Now write down several qualities or attributes that make this special person such a good stress manager.

2) The trainer invites participants to introduce themselves to others in the group.

➤ Each person takes a turn. Explain who your stress model is and describe in a few sentences the characteristics you would like to emulate in your model (eg, how you cope, attitude, level of stress).

3) The trainer may summarize the insights of the group and use them as a springboard for an in-depth presentation on successful coping styles.

Introduction B: UNDER FIRE

1) The trainer leads participants in the first round of introductions.

➤ Find a partner and a private space in the room.

➤ Introduce yourselves and take a few minutes to share one or two situations that you find particularly stressful.

2) The trainer calls time and invites each pair to find another pair and join in a foursome. Once the small groups of four are settled, the trainer announces that the next ten minutes will be spent in an intergroup contest. She distributes a matchbook to each group and describes the process in detail:

➤ Each group will generate a list of stressors.

➤ The youngest person in each group will be given a book of matches. Take a match, light it, hold it and name as many stressors as possible before the match burns out. Someone else in the group should keep track of the stressors named.

➤ No additional stressors may be added after the match goes out. Only the person holding the match may contribute ideas to the list.

➤ The next older person in the group will then light the next match and name as many different stressors as you can before the match goes out. Someone in the group should record all the new stressors, eliminating duplicates.

➤ The process will be repeated until all have taken a turn. Each person gets only one opportunity.

➤ A prize will be awarded to the group that comes up with the most stressors.

3) At a signal from the trainer, the groups begin.

4) As soon as all groups have finished, the trainer asks for a report on the total number of stressors named by each group and presents an appro-

priate small prize to the winning foursome (eg, sugarless gum, an empty bottle of "stresstabs," aloe leaves for burnt fingers, etc).

5) The trainer invites participants to reflect on the pressure they felt while completing this exercise—and to spend 5 minutes in their foursomes sharing reactions to questions such as:

✔ What was the most stressful part of this exercise?

✔ What physical or emotional symptoms of stress did you experience?

✔ Do you experience similar symptoms when feeling hurried, on the spot or under pressure at work, at home or in social situations?

6) The trainer reconvenes the entire group and asks for comments about how people respond differently under pressure and for observations about the wide variety of symptoms they experience when under stress.

TRAINER'S NOTES

Models was submitted by Pat Miller. ***Under Fire*** was submitted by Mark Warner.

74 AGENDA CONSENSUS

Participants use notecards to record their own expectations for the meeting, then compare notes with others in the group and identify which personal goals will and won't be met.

GOALS

To identify and articulate personal goals.

To build group cohesion.

To clarify what will not be covered in the meeting.

GROUP SIZE

Works best with fewer than 30 people.

TIME FRAME

15 minutes

MATERIALS

Several 3"x5" index cards for each participant; tape; blackboard or newsprint easel.

PROCESS

1) The trainer introduces the exercise, covering some or all of the following points.

   ● The subject of stress usually attracts people with all sorts of hopes and expectations.

   ● Often we are not consciously aware of the variety of goals we have for a learning experience and are vaguely disappointed when these unspoken agendas are not fulfilled.

   ● Usually we don't know if our needs are going to be met until the event has been completed.

2) The trainer explains that this exercise will allow everyone to have some input into what happens during the meeting and will also clarify which issues are outside the scope of this experience.

3) The trainer distributes 3"x5" cards to participants and invites them to reflect on their expectation for the learning experience.

➤ What do you hope to learn or accomplish in this workshop (class/ retreat/meeting)? Write one goal on each card.

☞ *While participants are writing goals, make a consensus poster with two sections, one labeled* **Will Be Met partially or in full** *and the other labeled* **Won't Be Met—need other resources.** *Be sure to have plenty of tape for securing all the cards to the poster.*

4) After most people have written their goals, the trainer collects all the cards, shuffles them thoroughly to insure anonymity and reads them one by one. As he reads each one, he comments on whether or not it will be met during the learning experience and tapes it to the appropriate poster.

➤ Agendas that will be covered *for sure* are posted in the **Will Be Met** section.

➤ Agendas that may be met *only partially* are noted, explained and posted in the **Will Be Met** section.

➤ Agendas that will *definitely not* be covered in the meeting are posted in the **Won't Be Met** section. The trainer explains why they will not be met and gives suggestions for how these goals could be met elsewhere.

Participants are also invited to write on these cards during break time, suggesting additional ways these goals could be met outside the session.

5) The trainer uses the **Will Be Met** goal cards to highlight the agenda for the remainder of the meeting and to introduce the first topic.

VARIATIONS

■ After *Step 3* participants could form trios, introduce themselves and share their goals and expectations. After 5–10 minutes the trainer asks each group to agree together on one goal they would all like to see accomplished during the meeting. These consensus goals are listed separately and incorporated into the trainer's agenda for the meeting.

Submitted by Jerry Glashagel.

©1994 Whole Person Press 210 W Michigan Duluth MN 55802   (800) 247-6789

75 MARAUDERS

This highly active and entertaining sensory awareness exercise demonstrates the physical symptoms of stress. Participants learn to recognize their own unique patterns of reaction to stress.

GOALS

To identify the body's physical response to stressful events.

To demonstrate how stress is triggered by both positive and negative events.

To enable participants to recognize their own unique symptoms of stress.

GROUP SIZE

Unlimited, as long as space is large enough.

TIME FRAME

20–30 minutes

MATERIALS

Blackboard or flipchart.

PROCESS

☞ *Since this activity involves unexpected and unsolicited touching, use it with discretion. Encourage folks to participate only at their personal comfort level. Same sex groups may be more appropriate; or offer an option to to serve as group observers.*

1) The trainer introduces the exercise by pointing out the following facts about stress.

   ● The stress response is a physical reaction—the body's response to any demand for change.

   ● Although the mechanism is the same for everyone, each of us responds in a slightly different manner—some with sweaty palms, some with tense muscles and some with hyperventilating or a variety of other symptoms.

   ● Recognition of these early warning signs can help you alleviate the physical impact of stress before it becomes too great.

2) The trainer asks participants to stand and form small groups of six persons each and once they have gathered, gives instructions for setting up.

➤ Decide who will be the first marauder.

➤ The other people make a circle, facing each other with your eyes closed. The marauder should stay on the outside of the circle.

3) The trainer guides the group through **Round One**.

➤ Marauders—slowly and silently circle your group. After prowling around the circle once or twice, stop behind the person of your choice and startle her by suddenly yelling "HA!" while grabbing her sharply at the waist.

➤ The startled person will then become the new marauder while the previous marauder joins the circle. Everyone close your eyes and get ready for the next "attack."

Throughout the exercise, the trainer gives continuous verbal guidelines to the circle groups.

➤ Notice any body sensations that you are experiencing while waiting for the marauder to strike (eg, tight shoulder muscles, clenched jaws and fists, nervous stomach, shallow breathing);

➤ Refrain from judging these sensations—ie, whether you like or dislike them—instead get into the experience of them, focusing on just the sensations themselves;

➤ Pay attention to how you feel when you get "zapped" by a marauder—notice the sudden "rush" you experience.

   ☞ *The trainer needs to repeat these guidelines several times (perhaps each time the marauder switches) in order to keep participants focused on their bodily sensations throughout the exercise.*

   The process continues for about five minutes or until everyone in the group has had a chance to become a marauder.

4) After about five minutes the trainer calls a halt to the exercise, but asks people to remain in their groups for **Round Two.**

➤ Now we are going to repeat the exercise, except this time the marauder should replace the startle routine with a gentle and soothing massage of the neck and shoulders of your chosen "victim."

   ☞ *Again, the groups should continue to switch marauders until everyone has had at least one turn to give a massage.*

Throughout this phase of the session the trainer offers continuing verbal guidance.

➤ Notice any anticipatory physical symptoms you may be feeling while waiting for the marauder to select you.

➤ Pay attention to your immediate reaction when first touched.

➤ Notice any subsequent physical sensations when your neck and shoulders are massaged.

5) After five minutes the trainer again calls time, asking the groups to stay put for **Round Three.**

➤ Let's try the exercise one last time, with a new set of rules.

➤ This time the marauder has a choice—you may either startle (grab) or soothe (massage) the person in the circle.

☞ *The process continues as before with each new marauder selecting a "victim" and choosing to soothe or startle that person.*

The trainer periodically directs participants to become aware of whatever physical sensations they are experiencing in anticipation of the marauder, using suitable prompts such as:

➤ Whether you are startled or soothed, notice how you react when you are first touched.

➤ Pay attention to your physical responses after you have been touched.

6) **Processing the information.** The trainer asks participants to describe the physical sensations they experienced during the exercise and records their comments on the flip chart.

✔ How did you feel waiting for it to happen? Upset? Embarrassed? Foolish? Angry?

✔ Where did you notice areas of tension in your body?

✔ What other sensations did you experience?

✔ How did you feel about being touched?

✔ Was there any difference between anticipating shock versus pleasure?

7) The trainer helps participants generalize by asking them to identify similarities between how they reacted during the exercise and how they experience stress in daily life. To facilitate discussion, the trainer poses one or both of the following questions:

✔ Describe some of your typical stress reactions and what triggers them.

✔ What value is there in being able to recognize the physical signs of stress?

8) The trainer may want to close the experience by leading participants in a stretching or relaxation exercise to put the group at ease.

TRAINER'S NOTES

Submitted by Joseph J Giacalone.

76 PANDORA'S BOX

Participants get acquainted as they identify major sources of stress and discover a surprise ending.

GOALS

To identify personal stressors and promote self-awareness.

To promote group cohesion.

GROUP SIZE

Best with a group of 6–12 people; with larger audiences, divide into small groups for *Steps 1–4*.

TIME FRAME

Approximately 15 minutes. Discussion may last up to 30 minutes, depending on the depth and direction dictated by the needs/interests of participants.

MATERIALS

A gift box (Pandora's Box!) lined with a paper on which is written the word "HOPE" (make the letters large enough to be seen by the whole group); small slips of paper (two or three for each participant); pencils.

PROCESS

1) The trainer distributes two or three paper slips to everyone and gives instructions.

   ➤ Write one personal stressor on each slip of paper you have been given.

2) Participants put their stressors into Pandora's Box.

3) The trainer opens Pandora's Box, chooses a slip of paper, reads the stressor written there and invites participants to share their feelings and reactions to this stressor.

4) The trainer reads the remaining stressors one at a time and encourages discussion about the impact such experiences have in people's lives.

5) When all stressors have been identified and discussed, the trainer shows everyone that one thing remains in the box—HOPE!

6) The trainer points out the importance of hope and positive attitude in managing stress, noting that this learning experience is an opportunity for participants to open their own Pandora's Box and discover renewed hope for dealing with the distress they may find there.

☞ *This exercise serves as a perfect springboard for an exploration of various means of coping with stress and distress.*

VARIATIONS

■ This exercise is also effective as an introduction to a session designed to prevent or explore staff burnout issues.

TRAINER'S NOTES

Submitted by Marcia A Schnorr, RN, MS. Based on a group exercise designed by psychiatric nursing students.

77 TRAVELING TRIOS

In this fast-paced icebreaker participants move from group to group, meeting each other and describing their coping styles.

GOALS

To reflect on and affirm personal styles of managing stress.

To make positive contact with many other participants.

GROUP SIZE

Works best with 16 or more people.

TIME FRAME

10–15 minutes

PROCESS

1) The trainer asks participants to stand and gather in one area of the room. As soon as all are assembled, the trainer guides the group through the first step of the mixer.

   ➤ Find two other people whose names have at least one letter in common with yours.

   ☞ *If the participants don't divide evenly into trios, make one or two groups of four rather than a group of two.*

   ➤ Introduce yourself to your two partners and share something about your style of managing stress. You will have 2 minutes for this initial introduction, so make sure you learn something about each person during that time.

2) After 2 minutes the trainer calls time (a harmonica or whistle works well, especially in a large group) and gives instructions for the next trio.

   ➤ The oldest person in each group should leave and "cut in" on another group to form a new trio.

   ➤ In this new group, introduce yourself again and briefly describe some other dimension of your coping style. Do not repeat yourself. The information must be completely different from what you shared with your previous group.

   ➤ Take 2 minutes to get acquainted.

3) After 2 minutes the trainer calls time again and gives instructions for the third trio.

> ➤ The tallest person in each group should leave and find a new trio.

> ➤ In this new group, describe still other aspects of your stress management style.

4) *Step 3* is repeated several times without participants repeating any information.

> ☞ *Use unusual, humorous criteria to determine which person leaves the group (eg, the straightest teeth, the biggest car, came from furthest away, shortest hair, longest fingers, etc).*

5) When the group's energy begins to flag, the trainer instructs people to return to their seats and write a paragraph about their personal coping style as they described it during this exercise.

6) The trainer invites all who choose to read their paragraphs. She then moves into a more detailed presentation on strategies for coping with stress.

> ☞ *The **AAAbc's of Stress Management** (Stress 1, p 49), **Coping Skills Assessment** (Stress 1, p 63), **PILEUP Copers** (Stress 2, p 54), and **S.O.S. for Stress** (Stress 3, p 54) would be good follow-ups to this exercise.*

78 GOING TO JERUSALEM

Participants use stress symptoms to play an old-fashioned icebreaker.

GOALS

To get acquainted.

To identify symptoms of stress.

GROUP SIZE

Up to 20. With more people, divide into groups of 8–16.

TIME FRAME

10–20 minutes

PROCESS

1) The trainer notes that this icebreaker will be familiar to most people and asks for a volunteer to explain the normal rules.

   ➤ One person begins by saying, *"I'm going to Jerusalem and I'm taking an apple"* (or any other object that begins with the letter "A").

   ☞ *Feel free to change the pilgrimage city to match your group's cultural context. You could all use a neutral or humorous destination (eg, Hoboken or stress management course)*

   ➤ The next person repeats what the first person said and adds her own item, this time beginning with the letter "B." *"I'm going to Jerusalem and I'm taking an apple and a balloon."*

   ➤ The next in line recalls the previous items and adds something beginning with the letter "C."

   ➤ This process is repeated by each participant in turn until the group has covered the whole alphabet.

2) The trainer announces that for this game the airlines have limited the baggage that may be taken to Jerusalem and are instead requiring all passengers to name a symptom of stress before they board.

   ☞ *If the group is unfamiliar with the concept of stress symptoms, you may want to stop here for a brief presentation on physical, emotional, interpersonal and spiritual symptoms. Elicit examples from the group and supplement them with ideas from the list below.*

---

3) After the group is warmed up to the concept, the trainer invites people to play this modified version of **Going to Jerusalem**:

> ➤ Someone starts by introducing herself and the stress symptom beginning with the letter "A" that she is taking to Jerusalem (eg, *"I'm Sue and I'm anxious"*).

> ➤ The second person introduces himself, recalls the "A" stress symptom, and then adds a "B" symptom of his own (eg, *"I'm Stuart and I'm anxious and bulemic"*).

> ➤ The process continues around the group until all have had a turn. If anyone gets stuck, the trainer should invite others to brainstorm stress symptoms beginning with that letter.

4) In conclusion, the trainer invites comments from the group on the variety of symptoms that may be related to stress.

VARIATIONS

■ Participants could name sources of stress or choose coping resources instead of listing symptoms.

TRAINER'S NOTES

STRESS SYMPTOMS

A anxiety, apprehension, addiction, arguments, apathy, abuse.

B boredom, back-biting, backache, blues, blahs.

C colds, canker sores, claustrophobia, compulsiveness, crying spells, cynicism, clamming up, conflict, confusion.

D drinking, drugs, depression, diarrhea, divorce, distrust, defensiveness.

E edginess, emptiness.

F fear, forgetfulness, flu, fatigue, frustration, flush.

G guilt, gas, grudges.

H hopelessness, heart attack, high blood pressure, headaches.

I indigestion, insomnia, irritability, irrational thoughts, indecision, intolerance.

J judgmental stance, joylessness, jitters.

K know-it-all attitude, knots in stomach or back.

L loneliness, lowered libido, lethargy, lashing out, lack of concentration.

M muscle twitches, martyrdom, mood swings.

N nagging, negative attitude, nightmares, nervousness, needing to prove something.

O orneriness, out of touch, out of control.

P panic, pounding heart, put downs, poor judgment, pushing too hard.

Q quiet, quick to take offense, questioning.

R rudeness, rash (skin), resentment, righteous indignation.

S sulking, stewing, spiritual void, self-recriminations.

T temper tantrums, too much to do, tension, trouble setting priorities.

U unhappiness, unforgiving spirit, uncertainty, unproductive approach to work, unrealistic expectations.

V volatile, vague aches & pains, values confusion.

W weight gain/loss, whirling mind, worrying, wasting time.

X x-tra pounds, x-travagant living.

Y yelling, yawns, yah-buts.

Z zillions of things undone, zero energy.

©1994 Whole Person Press 210 W Michigan Duluth MN 55802   (800) 247-6789

Stress
Assessments

79 SPICE OR ARSENIC?

Using an unusual measuring device, participants assess current and past stress levels and decide how much is enough for them.

GOALS

To assess personal stress levels.

To explore individual variation in healthy stress levels.

GROUP SIZE

Unlimited.

TIME FRAME

20–30 minutes

MATERIALS

Stress Thermometer worksheet for everyone.

PROCESS

1) The trainer begins with a general introduction to stress covering information such as:
   - Stress is universal.
   - Stress is not all bad. In fact, we need a certain amount of stress to be vibrant, lively, productive people.
   - Too much stress can be disastrous. In large doses the "spice" of life can poison us.
   - How much is too much? Healthful stress levels vary greatly from individual to individual. Your optimal stress level is different from others in this room! The key question is "What is the best level for you?"

2) The trainer distributes the **Stress Thermometer** and invites participants to assess the stress in their lives.
   > List at the top of the page all the sources of stress in your life right now.

   > ☞ *To prime the pump, solicit several examples from the group or list a variety of stressors. Allow plenty of time for people to recall and note their stressors.*

➤ Now assess your present stress level by filling in the thermometer on the left to the level that seems to best represent your current life situation.

➤ Now respond to the two additional questions at the bottom of the worksheet:

    ➤ Is this level spice or arsenic for you?

    ➤ Is your stress level stable, rising or falling?

3) The trainer announces that there is an imaginary stress thermometer running down the middle of the room with "I QUIT" on one end, "ZZZZZ" on the other, and the various levels spaced in between.

    ☞ *You may want to prepare signs or placards to mark and identify the location of the different stress levels in the room.*

Participants are invited to explore their stress further using this room-sized version of the thermometer.

➤ Stand up, take your and pencils along, and move to the place on this giant thermometer that represents the personal stress level that you marked on your worksheet thermometer.

    ☞ *Make sure everyone has found an appropriate place before continuing.*

➤ Everyone experiencing the same stress level should form a group.

    ☞ *If some groups are too small, combine groups in adjacent stress levels. If a group is too large (more than 8 people), divide it into smaller units.*

➤ Introduce yourselves and discuss what symptoms of stress are typical for you at this level.

4) After about 5 minutes, the trainer interrupts and asks participants to think back to one year ago, and assess their stress level at that time.

➤ Mark your stress level on the corresponding worksheet thermometer.

➤ Then move to the appropriate level on the room-size continuum.

    ☞ *Once everyone is settled at their new location, ask for a show of hands in response to the following questions.*

✔ How many people were at a higher stress level a year ago?

✔ How many were at a lower stress level?

✔ How many haven't changed in a year?

5) The trainer invites participants to place themselves on the thermometer one more time.

©1994 Whole Person Press 210 W Michigan Duluth MN 55802   (800) 247-6789

➤ Reflect on the stress level you would like to be experiencing six months from now.

➤ Record your level on the appropriate worksheet thermometer.

➤ Move once again, relocating to the spot in the room that corresponds to your desired level.

☞ *Wait until everyone has found a spot.*

➤ The people at each stress level once again form groups and discuss what steps you will need to take in order to reach (or maintain) this stress level.

6) The trainer reconvenes the whole group and asks for insights and observations.

☞ *You may also wish to point out that a stress management course is not designed to completely eliminate stress—thus producing a room full of "ZZZZZs!" Rather, it is supposed to help each person move toward the level of stress that seems appropriate to that person. Therefore, if a course is to be successful, participants must keep their own personal goals in mind.*

VARIATIONS

■ Participants could complete the Holmes and Rahe *Social Readjustment Rating Scale* prior to *Step 2*. During *Step 5* people in each small group compare notes on their scores. This provides a perfect opportunity to point out that the same amount of change may provoke different levels of stress in different people.

*Adapted from DA Tubesing, **Stress Skills** (Duluth MN: Whole Person Associates, 1978).*

STRESS THERMOMETER

MY PRESENT STRESS

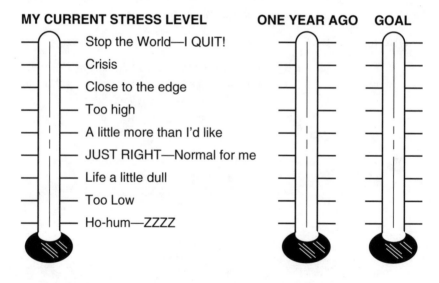

MY CURRENT STRESS LEVEL

— Stop the World—I QUIT!

— Crisis

— Close to the edge

— Too high

— A little more than I'd like

— JUST RIGHT—Normal for me

— Life a little dull

— Too Low

— Ho-hum—ZZZZ

ONE YEAR AGO   GOAL

Is your current level of stress SPICE or ARSENIC?

Is your stress level: ___ stable   ___ rising   ___ falling

---

80 ON THE SPOT

In this thought-provoking process participants examine situations in which they are most vulnerable to manipulations and, using **Ten Steps to Critical Thinking,** brainstorm ways to avoid being manipulated in the future.

GOALS

To increase awareness of the stress of manipulation.

To apply critical thinking techniques as a stress management strategy in potentially manipulative situations.

GROUP SIZE

Unlimited.

TIME FRAME

30–60 minutes

MATERIALS

Paper and writing utensils; **Manipulation Patterns** for everyone.

PROCESS

1) The trainer announces that this exercise will help participants assess their vulnerability to being manipulated by others and by situations. He introduces the concept of "mind control" and describes how such manipulation occurs, using the following notes as guidelines.

   ● Mind control is a form of social influence that is both stressful and unethical, since it restricts freedom of choice by *manipulating* people to act in ways they did not intend.

   ● Usually when we think of mind control, we think of brainwashing or shock treatment or hypnosis—traumas which most of us, fortunately, never experience. But unfortunately, mind control is a much more common experience. **We all experience it every day**—in all kinds of situations—when we are consciously or unconsciously manipulated into doing or saying something that we really didn't choose freely. Such manipulation is fostered by three major forces: demand situations, other people and our own expectations.

- **Situations and roles that demand a certain behavior** from us are inherently manipulative. All of us respond to these *demand* characteristics in situations and relationships—often without questioning, or even noticing. For example,
  - ○ *Guests . . . don't complain;*
  - ○ *Big boys . . . don't cry;*
  - ○ *Team players . . . cooperate;*
  - ○ *Interviewees . . . answer questions;*
  - ○ *Children . . . do as they are told;*
  - ○ *Men . . . protect women;*
  - ○ *Women . . . are "ladylike."*

  These and hundreds of other expectations that people *should behave* in a certain way control our behavior and limit our choices.

- **Other people who want us to do something** exert a form of mind control. They beg, threaten, pout, cajole, sweet talk, push, lay on guilt, get mad or sad—and adopt hundreds of other clever postures designed to get us to do what *they* want rather than what *we* want.

- **Our own mind games** foster manipulation. We set ourselves up for being controlled by our expectations, by what we tell ourselves, by what we believe, by our sense of morality and responsibility, by our knowledge of our shortcomings and mistakes, etc. Self-talk such as, "I must please everyone," "I don't deserve much," "I really should have done xxxxx," "I need to be perfect," "I'm really very weak," etc, makes us particularly vulnerable to manipulation by others.

- Most of us develop personal patterns of vulnerability to specific types of manipulation. We can easily see through and resist some mind control forces, while repeatedly falling easy prey to other manipulations that "push our buttons!"

- Whatever the reason you lose or let go of control, *you* are the only one who can get it back—only you can take control again.

2) The trainer distributes a **Manipulation Patterns** worksheet to everyone and guides participants through the process, one section at a time.

  ☞ *For each section, read out loud the question at the left, give an example or two, then allow a few minutes for participants to write their examples. Finally, pose the corresponding "hooker" questions, give an example or two and wait a moment for people to write their responses.*

> *After repeating this process for the four manipulation questions, encourage participants to summarize their insights and uncover their personal vulnerability themes using the prompts in the boxes at the bottom of the worksheet.*

3) The trainer asks participants to form groups of three for discussion.

> ➤ Get together with two people you know least well.

> ➤ Take turns sharing your stories and "most vulnerable characteristics" with each other. Each person should take about 3 minutes to describe situations when you were manipulated, giving details about why and how it happened.

4) After 10 minutes the trainer interrupts with instructions for group brainstorming.

> ➤ Each group of three should now list on newsprint the most troublesome situations that "push your buttons," and the personality characteristics that make you most vulnerable to manipulation.

> ➤ Once you have a lengthy list, go back and brainstorm a corresponding list of clever ways each situation could be handled more efficiently so that the manipulation is avoided.

> ☞ *Encourage participants' creativity by noting that many suggestions may be humorous—and that such out-of-the-ordinary approaches are often the most helpful.*

5) The trainer reconvenes the large group and invites participants to share examples of their vulnerability as well as some of the best ideas they came up with for taking control of their actions and thwarting the manipulations they experience.

> ☞ *People may need a gentle reminder to share only their own stories and not comment on those of others.*

> *Model the sharing process by giving an example of your own— or adapt this one:*

> > *I am easily made to feel guilty. If I see someone I have not called or written to in a year, I try to avoid them. Then if they say, "How come you haven't called?" I feel guilty. One solution is to practice first saying to **them**, "Why haven't you called?" They will handle the guilt much better than I will, I reason.*

> > *After I've practiced that for awhile, I will **graduate** to being able to hear someone else say "Why haven't you called?"*

---

without the guilt which leaves me open to manipulation, and I'll be able to answer, "Yes, we've both been so busy we haven't been able to get together!" Now it's not a game of who can be first, but the responsibility is shared.

6) As people share their examples, the trainer comments briefly and points out how each alternative solution illustrates one of the **Ten Steps To Critical Thinking** which he outlines on the board as the ideas arise:

- **Recognize demand characteristics.** Rethink the expectations which seem implicit in situations and relationships. Is it necessary for experts to always be sure of themselves? Should soldiers always follow orders? And must dinner invitations always be reciprocated in kind? You don't always have to do what's expected!

- **Remember, you can say NO!**

- **Recognize false dilemmas**. Always add "none of the above" to any multiple choice!

- **Sleep on it.** Recognize pressure to decide quickly. Don't act under stress.

- **Look for the hidden agenda.** What is really being said? What is not being said? To whom, by whom and why is it being said?

- **Recognize logical fallacies**. Be especially cautious of any "appeal" to your "sense of logic."

- **Know who you're dealing with**. Ask blunt questions and do not accept vague answers. Find out what a person represents.

- **Recognize flattery.**

- **Ask questions**. Challenge authority claims.

- **Retain your self worth.** Whatever happens, say "I'm great!" Don't be afraid to be different.

7) After several people have shared their stories, the trainer concludes by summarizing strategies for avoiding the subtle, everyday pressures of mind control and coping with the stress of vulnerability.

Submitted by Bob Fellows.

©1994 Whole Person Press 210 W Michigan Duluth MN 55802   (800) 247-6789

MANIPULATION PATTERNS
how I set myself up to be taken advantage of

When have you been convinced to buy something you didn't really want? Jot down one or two examples.	What hooked you? What feelings set you up to be manipulated?
When have you accepted a drink, drug, or even some food when you didn't really want it? Jot down some examples.	What hooked you? What about you contributed to your action?
When have you felt manipulated or "taken advantage of?" Remember several instances and jot down a note about each.	How did you set yourself up to be taken advantage of?
When have you verbally agreed to something that you didn't believe was true? Recall one or two instances.	Why didn't you speak your mind?

SUMMARY THEMES: look over your examples for insights

What would you say generally "pushes your buttons"and gets you to do something you did not want to do?	If a member of this group wanted to take advantage of you, how could they best do it?
What is your most vulnerable characteristic that sets you up to be manipulated?	

81 DRAINERS AND ENERGIZERS

The checklists used in this exercise prompt participants to identify the negative stressors in their lives that drain them, as well as the positive energizers that refill them—at work, at home and at play.

GOALS

To identify the daily drainers that deplete energy.

To recognize and utilize the daily energizers that restore vitality.

GROUP SIZE

Unlimited; the group brainstorming in *Step 2* is best done with 20–80 people.

TIME FRAME

10–25 minutes

MATERIALS

One copy of **Daily Drainers** and **Personal Energizers** worksheet for each participant.

PROCESS

1) The trainer instructs participants to fill in the boxes of the **Daily Drainers** worksheet. (4–5 minutes)

   ➤ List all the minor stressful irritants that occur to you in the various areas of your life. You don't have to fill every box. Two or three items will probably come quickly to mind for some categories, while other categories may end up empty.

2) When most people have completed the worksheet, the trainer highlights one category at a time and solicits from the group 3 or 4 examples for each type of drainer.

   ☞ *Encourage participants to expand their personal list by adding those suggestions of others that particularly apply to them.*

3) Participants look over their lists and note the settings in which most of their stress-producing drainers occur (home, work or play).

4) *Steps 1, 2* and *3* are repeated using the **Personal Energizers** worksheet.

5) After participants have shared and analyzed how and where they get revitalized, the trainer encourages people to compare their two lists.

➤ Reflect on the *balance* of drainers and energizers in the different contexts of your life (home, work and play).

➤ Record your insights on the back of one of the worksheets.

6) The trainer solicits observations, reactions and insights from the group.

7) In closing the trainer points out that one way to decrease the risk of stress exhaustion is to increase your daily dose of revitalizing energizers. She then invites participants to make a mini-plan for revitalization.

➤ Identify one energizer you want to utilize more frequently in each life context—at home, at work and at play.

VARIATIONS

■ If time is short, either the **Drainers** or **Energizers** worksheet can be used alone.

■ For use as an icebreaker, the trainer chooses a specific box from the worksheet (eg, something that annoys you where you work) and asks participants to pair up, introduce themselves and share the items they wrote in that space. After a moment or two, people are instructed to find a new partner, exchange names and share their responses to a different item from the drainer or energizer worksheet, as designated by the trainer. This process is repeated several times, each time with a new partner and a different answer box.

■ After *Step 5* participants could form and discuss their reactions to the worksheets, sharing their insights about the most surprising responses or general themes that emerged.

Excerpted from Tubesing, Sippel and Tubesing, **Personal Recharging: Rx for Burnout in the Workplace** *(Duluth MN: Whole Person Press, 1981).*

PERSONAL DRAINERS

Activities/Conditions/ Places/People that...	AT HOME	AT WORK	AT PLAY
ANNOY ME			
ANGER ME			
DISTRACT ME			
DEPRESS ME			
WORRY ME			
WEAR ME OUT			
BORE ME			
FRUSTRATE ME			
PLAGUE ME			

PERSONAL FILLERS

Activities/Conditions/ Places/People that...	AT HOME	AT WORK	AT PLAY
EXCITE ME			
CALM ME			
FREE ME			
BRING ME JOY			
SUPPORT/ NURTURE ME			
STIMULATE/ CHALLENGE ME			
GIVE ME MEANING			
MAKE ME LAUGH			
ENERGIZE ME			

82 LIFE TRAP 3: SICK OF CHANGE

In this multi-phase exercise participants examine the role of change in their lives and the stress it creates. The double assessment, both objective and subjective, allows them ample opportunity to explore their current risk level and to articulate with each other the nature of the changes they are experiencing. Finally, participants plan strategies for taking charge of their own level and pace of change as they move into the future.

GOALS

To understand the connection between stress, life changes and health.

To assess the levels and types of change present in current life situations.

To explore strategies for managing the stress of change.

GROUP SIZE

Unlimited.

TIME FRAME

60–90 minutes

MATERIALS

Blank paper; one copy of the **Change Checklist** and **Changes and Personal Outlook** worksheets for each participant.

PROCESS

☞ *This is a five-part exercise:*

A) *1–2–3 Change: Warm-up chalktalk with sharing in pairs. (10–15 minutes)*

B) *The Change Factor: Chalktalk on change, stress and illness. (10–15 minutes)*

C) *Exploring the Meaning of Change: Subjective assessment. (10 minutes)*

D) *Small Group Sharing: (15–25 minutes)*

E) *Taking Charge of Change: Wrap-up exploring strategies for coping with change and personal planning for anticipated change. (15-25 minutes)*

A. 1–2–3 Change: Introductory Warm-Up (10–15 minutes)

☞ *At the beginning of this session you may want to play music that reflects the theme of change and sets the mood of this exercise (eg, "Everything Changes," or "Turn, Turn," etc).*

1) The trainer introduces the subject of change and the process of the session.

- **Change is a part of life**—there is no escaping it! And since change always requires us to adapt, it always causes stress.
- **Change can provide the spice of life.** Without the stimulation of change—new challenges, new experiences, new relationships—life would be rather dull. Who would refuse a promotion or avoid a marriage or not have children just because it might be stressful?
- On the other hand, research shows that **too much change can drain** our coping reserves—and it can make us sick!
- This session will help you explore change both from an objective and from a subjective, personal view as you seek to discover the kind and amount of change that works best for you.

2) The trainer distributes blank paper to participants and asks them to reflect on the following questions.

☞ *Read the questions one at a time, giving a wide range of examples to stimulate discussion. Allow ample time for participants to answer each question before moving on to the next.*

➤ Think about all the changes that have occurred for you during the past year. Please write down three things that you chose to change—of your own free will (eg, career, living accommodations, work schedule, new car, redecorating, hair style, etc).

➤ Now make note of three changes that occurred to you, about which you had *no choice*, over which you had no control (eg, death, local grocery closed, trip canceled due to weather, your injured back, a friend moved, etc).

➤ Next list three changes you would *like to make* in the future (eg, be less impatient, write more letters, get a new job, retire, get married, save more money, volunteer somewhere, etc).

➤ Please look over your list of nine changes and note which was (or would be) most difficult for you.

➤ Which change was (or is) most desirable?

➤ Which one caused you (or probably will cause you) the most stress?

3) The trainer directs participants to pair up with a neighbor and share some of the experiences and responses that were elicited by these questions. (5 minutes)

4) After the total group has been reconvened people are invited to share a few observations and insights on the nature of change in their lives and their varied reactions to it.

B. The Change Factor: Objective Assessment (10-15 minutes)

☞ *The concepts and worksheet in this section are based on the research of Holmes and Rahe at the University of Washington. Their "Social Readjustment Rating Scale" could be substituted for the worksheet here.*

5) The trainer expands on the relationship between stress and change, covering some or all of the following points:

● Endocrinologist, Hans Selye, coined the word **stress** to describe a phenomenon he observed and studied in his research. He defined stress as, "The non-specific response of the body to any demand placed on it."

● From this definition we can conclude that life is inherently stressful because it is full of change. Any change requires adaptation and therefore puts demands on our body systems.

● Every year all of us experience a wide variety of life changes— predictable events like a child going away to college, as well as unexpected occurrences such as a job layoff or winning the lottery!

● While some of these changes may seem positive or desirable and others negative, research indicates that they are all stressful!

6) The trainer distributes the **Change Checklist** worksheet to participants and guides them through the process of filling it out.

➤ First mark each life event you have experienced **during the past year.** (If the event has happened more than once, you should indicate the number of times.)

☞ *Wait until nearly everyone is finished before giving the next instruction.*

➤ Read through the list again, marking with a star (*) those life events that were **particularly stressful** to you—and then answer the questions at the bottom of the worksheet.

7) As people are finishing up the trainer polls the group, asking for a show of hands in response to the following additional questions:

✔ How many experienced none of the listed life events this last year?

✔ How many experienced 5 or less?

✔ How many 10 or more?

✔ How many 15 or more?

8) The trainer summarizes research findings on the relationship between change, stress and sickness, covering some or all of the points below.

- Whatever the source, **change is stressful by its very nature**. When too many changes occur too fast, we put excessive strain on our system. As we struggle to adapt we may feel depressed, get physically sick or make foolish decisions.

- Research into the relationships between life change, stress and health supports the common sense notion that **change takes its toll**. Studies at the University of Washington have demonstrated four attributes of change.

  ○ **Some changes consistently cause more stress than others.** The death of a young child is more stressful than a financial reversal, a divorce more stressful than a job change.

  ○ **Both positive and negative changes are stressful.** Both of them call for system-wide adaptation. A promotion can be just as stressful as a demotion.

  ○ **Changes tend to come in clusters,** creating a momentum of their own—one change leads to another. The stress also escalates, of course, as one adaptation demands another.

  ○ **An accumulation of changes over time,** or a large number of changes in a brief period, **increases stress**—and the risk of physical illness.

C. Meaning of Change: Subjective Assessment (10 minutes)

9) The trainer distributes **Changes and Personal Outlook** to everyone and guides them through the reflection and writing process, giving several examples at each step.

➤ Select from your **Change Checklist** worksheet one *high stress change* and one *low stress change* that has occurred recently and write these changes in the appropriate boxes at the top of your **Changes and Personal Outlook** worksheet.

➤ Reflect on each of these changes and record all the *adaptations*, major and minor adjustments that were required as a result of that change. (2–3 minutes)

➤ Consider your *perceptions* of that change and list them.

   ➤ How did you interpret the event?

   ➤ What meanings did you assign to it?

   ➤ What overall outlook did you use to view the event?

   ➤ What consequences did you imagine?

☞ *Encourage people to list all the extremes that occur to them.*

➤ Finally, analyze and summarize the relationships you see between your *interpretation* of each event and the *amount of stress* it caused you. Record your observations on the bottom of the worksheet.

D. Small Group Sharing and Discussion (15–25 minutes)

10) The trainer divides participants into groups of four people each, or invites them to rejoin small groups from earlier in the learning experience. Once everyone is settled, he gives instructions for discussion.

➤ Take five minutes each to share your summary of current life changes and the personal insights generated by the objective assessment (**Change Checklist**) and the subjective assessment (**Changes and Personal Outlook**) activities.

☞ *Announce that each participant may use the time in any way she chooses and may share in whatever way seems appropriate to her. The emphasis should be on allowing everyone her full five minutes to share and be heard.*

Encourage participants to listen as carefully as they can, and when their turn comes, to share as personally as they are willing.

11) The trainer reconvenes the total group and asks for general observations from participants before moving on.

E. Taking Charge: Coping Strategies (15–25 minutes)

12) The trainer notes that change is both unavoidable and desirable. But the stress of change can be minimized by managing it effectively.

The trainer facilitates a discussion on change management strategies by asking the group for suggestions on how best to manage change at home or on the job. As salient points emerge, he writes them on newsprint or the blackboard, asking for examples and amplifying the discussion as necessary.

13) If the following ideas for taking charge of change do not emerge during the course of the discussion, the trainer may want to interject them in his closing summary.

- **Take good care of yourself.** Build up your resistance by practicing positive health habits such as adequate rest, good nutrition, exercise, a regular schedule, etc.
- **Train for change.** Practice being flexible by taking different view-points, changing your routines periodically, trying something new each day or week.
- **Anticipate change.** Learn all you can about the potential or upcoming change. Imagine your responses to different options. Decide how you might best adjust. Plan for changes in advance whenever possible.
- **Avoid impulsive changes.** Evaluate all the pros and cons of changes you are considering. Anticipate problems and try to head them off in advance.
- **Build safety zones.** At times of major change or clusters of change, create a sanctuary for yourself with familiar routines and soothing environments. Maintain an oasis of stability.
- **Use a wide-angle lens.** Try to look at the broad view of your current situation. Put it in historical perspective—50 years from now, who will care? Learn from the past—"I know I'm a survivor!"
- **Be flexible.** Bend. Adapt. Flow with the necessary changes. Don't fight the inevitable. Allow the processes to unfold as they will—even when they take unexpected directions.
- **Explore change-related meanings and feelings.** Reflect on your own reactions to the change. Self-awareness is a powerful ally in times of stress.

- **Ask advice from veterans.** Consult with others who have survived the changes you are currently experiencing. Learn their management secrets.
- **Let yourself grieve.** Grief accompanies any change as we let go of a past treasure (or even a past pain in the neck) and move into the uncertainty of a new direction. Take time to grieve. No matter how insignificant the loss seems, grief is a healing process.
- **Pace yourself.** Don't hurry through the process of change. You'll just add to your stress! Give yourself time to recover and rest. Take your time making decisions.

14) As a concluding exercise, the trainer invites participants to plan ahead for managing a specific anticipated change. He asks everyone to reflect on the following questions, using the back of a worksheet to record their responses.

☞ *Ask the questions one at a time, pausing long enough between them so that people have ample opportunity to reflect and write.*

➤ As you look ahead and envision the changes you wish to make during the next few months—as well as those that will probably happen to you anyway—select one change that is likely to be troublesome for you. Write it down.

➤ What kind of adaptations and adjustments will you need to make because of that change? Record them.

➤ Describe the interpretations that will help you see this change in its most positive light.

➤ What coping skills and strategies will be particularly useful to you as you manage this change?

➤ How can you best prepare for this change? Make a few preliminary notes toward a working plan for dealing with the stress of this change.

15) If time allows, the trainer may invite participants to share their plans with a neighbor or with the whole group. He then may ask for reactions and insights to the issues raised during the entire exercise.

VARIATIONS

■ The "Social Readjustment Rating Scale" (Holmes, TH and RH Rahe [1967]. *Journal of Psychosomatic Research*, 11, 213–218) could be utilized as the worksheet for *Step 6* in place of the worksheet provided. Please note that Holmes & Rahe's scale is copyrighted and may not be duplicated without permission from their publisher, Pergamon Press (New York).

■ Portions of this exercise could be used separately if time does not allow for completion of the entire five-phase process.

TRAINER'S NOTES

CHANGE CHECKLIST*

Check the life changes you have experienced this year:

PERSONAL

- ❏ personal injury/illness, handicap
- ❏ pregnancy (yours or partner's)
- ❏ change in religious views/beliefs
- ❏ change in financial status
- ❏ change in self-concept
- ❏ ending a relationship
- ❏ change in emotional outlook
- ❏ change in roles
- ❏ buying/selling a car
- ❏ aging
- ❏ change in habits
    - ❏ alchohol   ❏ exercise
    - ❏ drugs   ❏ nutrition
    - ❏ tobacco
- ❏ other _____

FAMILY

- ❏ marriage
- ❏ family member(s) leaving home
- ❏ new family member(s)
- ❏ separation/divorce
- ❏ trouble with in-laws
- ❏ partner stopping/starting a job
- ❏ illness/healing of family member
- ❏ death of a close friend or family member
- ❏ parent/child tensions
- ❏ change in recreation patterns
- ❏ other _____
  _____

WORK

- ❏ changed work load
- ❏ change in play
- ❏ starting new job
- ❏ promotion/demotion
- ❏ retirement
- ❏ change in hours
- ❏ change in relationship at work
- ❏ change in job security
- ❏ strike
- ❏ change in financial status
- ❏ other _____
  _____

ENVIRONMENT

- ❏ natural disaster
- ❏ moving to a new:
    - ❏ house or apartment
    - ❏ neighborhood   ❏ climate
    - ❏ city   ❏ culture
- ❏ Christmas
- ❏ vacation
- ❏ remodeling
- ❏ war
- ❏ major house cleaning
- ❏ crime against property
- ❏ other _____
  _____

❏ Go back and mark the changes that required an extra adaptation because of their importance to you.

❏ Identify one change that had a surprising effect on you: _____

❏ How did it affect you? _____

*From D A Tubesing, **Kicking Your Stress Habits** (Duluth MN: Whole Person Associates, 1989).*

CHANGES AND PERSONAL OUTLOOK

DESCRIPTION	MY HIGH STRESS CHANGE	MY LOW STRESS CHANGE
STRESSFUL EVENT		
Adaptations Adjustments Other Changes Required		
Meanings Interpretations My Outlook		
In what ways does your interpretation of the change and what it will mean for you—your overall outlook—determine the amount of stress you will experience?		

83 JOB DESCRIPTIONS

Participants divide into separate male and female groups to examine how sex role stereotyping can lead to the interpersonal stress of conflicting expectations.

GOALS

To demonstrate role conflict as a source of stress.

To study role stereotypes that can cause stress and interfere with interpersonal communication.

To present attitude awareness as a technique in stress management.

GROUP SIZE

Designed for use in groups of 8 to 20 people, adaptable for larger groups. It works best with groups who are motivated to look at this issue in their work setting.

TIME FRAME

60 minutes

SETTING

Two adjoining rooms or a larger room with a divider so that two subgroups can meet privately.

MATERIALS

Two copies of the **Position Announcement** worksheet for each participant.

PROCESS

1) The trainer begins by distributing two copies of the **Position Announcement** to all participants and explaining that everyone will be asked individually and in groups to write two job descriptions—one for their own sex, and one for members of the opposite sex.

 ➤ Begin by using one **Position Announcement** outline to write a job description for the opposite sex. **Men** should describe the position requirements and qualifications for being "a woman." **Women** should set forth the requirements and qualifications for being "a man."

2) After 5–10 minutes the trainer announces that after he gives the next set of instructions, all the men will form one group and move to the adjacent room for their discussion. All the women will stay in this room and form their own discussion group.

☞ *During the entire process of Steps 2–4 men and women remain in separate work areas where they will not influence each other.*

The trainer describes the process each group will follow during the next 15 minutes:

➤ Designate one person as the group's recorder.

➤ Share the job descriptions you have written for the opposite sex.

➤ Based on these individual responses, each group should construct a composite "ideal" job description for the opposite sex. The *male* group constructs the "ideal" description for being a woman, the *female* group constructs the "ideal" description for being a man.

☞ *If possible, moderate one subgroup and use a colleague to moderate the other. If a subgroup is larger than 10 people, divide it into smaller discussion units to allow for more participation.*

3) After 15 minutes, the trainer announces to each group that the process of *Steps 1* and *2* are going to be repeated, except this time they will be asked to write and discuss job descriptions for members of their own sex.

➤ Take about 15 minutes to design a job description for your own sex.

➤ Each person write your own.

4) After 5–10 minutes, the trainer repeats the group instructions.

➤ Each group will now construct a "real" (not an "ideal") job description for your own sex. The *male* group develops a "real" description for men, the *female* group designs a "real" description for women.

5) The trainer reassembles the total group and asks the recorder from one group to read the "ideal" job description devised by their group for the opposite sex. The trainer asks the other group:

✔ How many of you feel you would qualify for this position, given the description?

6) The process of *Step 5* is repeated for the other group. The recorder reads the "ideal" description and members of the target group are polled on their suitability for the job.

©1994 Whole Person Press 210 W Michigan Duluth MN 55802   (800) 247-6789

7) The trainer elicits comments and reactions from both groups and facilitates a general discussion about gender role stereotyping and its stressful effects in interpersonal relationships.

8) Recorders from both groups read the "real" job descriptions composed by each sex and participants are asked to compare the real and ideal roles portrayed by these descriptions of the sexes.

9) The trainer invites participants to reflect on how they could use insights from this experience in managing stress better in their own lives. She solicits examples of specific applications and highlights the importance of attitude awareness in successful stress management.

VARIATIONS

■ This exercise could easily be adapted for other stress provoking role stereotype situations. Instead of composing "real" and "ideal" job descriptions for men and women, use roles such as parent/teenager, father/mother, worker/supervisor, executive/secretary, etc.

TRAINER'S NOTES

Submitted by Randy R Weigel.

POSITION ANNOUNCEMENT
Job Description

Position Title:

Major Responsibilities of Position:

Required Qualifications:

Desirable . . .

Must be Willing To . . .

Fringe Benefits:

84 THE LAST CHRISTMAS TREE

This fantasy exercise enables participants to explore the stress associ- ated with rejection. It is most effective at the beginning of a learning experience.

GOALS

To identify the stress of actual or potential rejection.

To stimulate discussion about the feelings of being "left out."

To discover alternative perceptions of the rejection experience.

GROUP SIZE

Works best with small groups (6–10 people), but can easily be adapted for larger or smaller groups.

TIME FRAME

20–30 minutes

MATERIALS

The Last Christmas Tree worksheets for everyone.

PROCESS

☞ *This experience may evoke strong feelings in some participants. If your group is too large or if your time frame is too short to respond compassionately to someone who vividly recollects a traumatic memory, modify the depth of this exercise by shortening the fantasy.*

1) The trainer introduces the exercise as a fantasy journey to explore one common source of stress—rejection. She invites participants to settle comfortably in their chairs and close their eyes.

☞ *For best effect, dim the lights and eliminate (or minimize) outside stimuli.*

2) As a warm-up, the trainer leads the group through any familiar breath-ing/relaxation sequence. (5 minutes)

3) Once everyone has settled down and relaxed, the trainer guides the group on an imaginary journey to a Christmas tree lot using The Last Christmas Tree script on page 47.

---

4) When several people have opened their eyes, the trainer distributes **Last Christmas Tree** worksheet to all. She invites participants to recall their visualization and jot down some notes about it.

➤ In *Area A*, write down any negative images or feelings that you remember from the visualization. How did it feel to be looked over and never taken—left for last? What stress did you experience?

➤ In *Area B*, record any positive images and feelings you noticed during the imaginary journey. Were there any good feelings or positive outcomes from the process of being left for last?

➤ In *Area C*, briefly outline your ending to the fantasy.

5) The trainer solicits examples of positive and negative feelings experienced by the group and uses these to stimulate discussion about the stress of rejection versus the possible advantages of perceiving this experience as being "set aside."

☞ *Be sure to note that everyone, at times, shares the experience of the rejected Christmas tree (eg, not being chosen for a team, no date for the prom, not getting a job, losing an election, feeling left out at a party).*

6) The trainer leads participants through the rest of the worksheet.

➤ Recall some of your own rejection experiences and make note of a few in *Area D* on the worksheet.

☞ *Pause until all have made a list.*

➤ Now look over your list of rejections, to remember how you coped with these situations.

➤ Jot down a phrase or two describing your coping styles for each rejection experience.

7) Each participant is invited to describe briefly his images during the visualization and then to read/share his ending. (5–10 minutes)

8) After everyone has had a turn, the trainer opens the floor to discussion of real life rejection experiences and how people have coped with them. (5–10 minutes)

☞ *For added interest, ask participants to consider how their ending to the visualization fits with their style of handling the stress of rejection.*

VARIATIONS

- Any similar visualization of potential rejection (eg, toys in a store, oranges on a peddler's cart, etc) could be substituted for the Christmas tree image.

- In a group of more than 8 people, divide into triads for sharing in *Steps 7* and *8*. Break the process into two segments and keep time for the groups—5 minutes to share stories and 5–10 minutes to explore rejection experiences and coping strategies.

Submitted by Marcia A Schnorr.

THE LAST CHRISTMAS TREE Script

Imagine you are a Christmas tree . . . waiting in the lot to be sold . . . .

Make your mental image as vivid and detailed as possible as you imagine yourselves in this place . . . .

> ☞ *This is an open fantasy experience. The questions are designed to set the scene and facilitate the visualization process. Give people plenty of time to play with the images in each segment.*

Picture the lot in your mind . . . .

Where is it? On a street corner? In a back yard? Out in the country? In a parking lot?

What time of day is it? What's the weather like? What can you smell? What do you see around you? What sounds do you hear?

What kind of tree are you? Spruce? Pine? Balsam? What size are you? What shape?

How many other trees are there with you? Are you thrown in a pile? Crowded in? Leaning on a brace? Or stuck in a snowbank?

> ☞ *When everyone seems involved in the fantasy, move on to the next sequence, pausing long enough after each image to let people really tune into the scene.*

Now imagine that many people are coming to examine the trees in the lot . . . .

Visualize each person walking up and down the rows . . . looking over the tress . . . making their selection . . . .

But you are not chosen . . . .

Notice how people decide which tree to buy . . . what do they say?

How do you feel as one-by-one, each of the other trees is selected and you are left behind, all alone—the last Christmas tree?

> ☞ *Don't rush. People will need time to experience the impact of not being picked.*

Take a few moments in silence to go with the flow of your imagination and then visualize a conclusion to your fantasy.

What happens next? How does the story end?

When you are finished, open your eyes.

THE LAST CHRISTMAS TREE

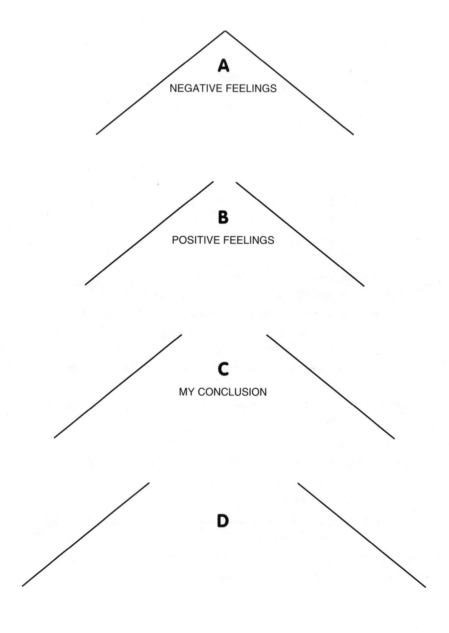

A
NEGATIVE FEELINGS

B
POSITIVE FEELINGS

C
MY CONCLUSION

D

Management
Strategies

85 METAPHORS

Participants study the form and function of various objects, seeking clues to creative stress management.

GOALS

To provide a model for back-home problem solving.

To promote creativity and non-linear approaches to stress management.

GROUP SIZE

Unlimited.

TIME FRAME

40–50 minutes

MATERIALS

Metaphors worksheets for all; a brown paper bag for each group, filled with 6–8 objects familiar to all participants (eg, file folders, transistor radio, car keys, ID badge, paycheck, telephone, toothbrush, paperclips, salt shaker, credit card, etc).

PROCESS

1) The trainer introduces the exercise by highlighting the importance of creativity in stressful situations—for changing perceptions and for generating alternative solutions.

   ● When we're stuck we can't think of new approaches for dealing with our stressors. Our lack of new ideas limits us and lowers our energy.

   ● **A new perspective can reduce stress and increase vitality** even if the situation itself doesn't change. New ideas almost always bring renewed energy for facing the problems that surround us.

   ● Common everyday items can stimulate our creativity by serving as **metaphors for coping**.

2) The trainer explains the process participants will learn for using everyday objects as metaphors to help manage stress.

   ● First we will notice and describe the **FORM** and **FUNCTION** of the item:

○ What is it like? How is it made? (*FORM*)
○ How is it used? What does it do? (*FUNCTION*)

● Next we ask the *force fit* question:
○ What can this item, with all its unique qualities, teach us about stress and how to manage it more effectively?

● This "force fit" generates new creative approaches to coping by stimulating a whole new mindset.

3) To illustrate this process the trainer chooses an object in the room (eg, piece of chalk) and asks participants to help describe characteristics of its design and *FORM*.

✔ What is this chalk like? How is it made?

☞ *Give some ideas to prime the pump (eg, cylindrical, smooth hard surface, fits easily in hand, flakes off on board but not on hands, color visible on contrasting background, brittle, etc).*

These attributes are recorded on the board. When 20 or more have been suggested, the trainer poses the *force fit metaphor* question:

✔ What can the FORM of this object teach us about stress and how to manage it better?

☞ *Possible responses: "Its cylindrical shape reminds us that we need to be well-rounded." "We, like the chalk, need a smooth hard surface so that criticism doesn't dent." "We need to show ourselves to good advantage by picking the background against which we shine." "Like brittle chalk we need a stiff backbone as well as a stiff upper lip." "Maybe I need to be more slippery—or grate on someone's nerves!"*

4) The trainer next asks the group to generate a list describing the possible *FUNCTIONS* of this object.

✔ How is this chalk used? What does it do?

☞ *Give some examples if needed (eg, draw hopscotch, record information on neutral surface, mark location for hemline, coat a plumbline, etc).*

After 15–20 functions are named, the trainer again poses the *force fit metaphor* question:

✔ How could these FUNCTIONS apply to stress and/or managing it better?

☞ *"When chalk is doing its job, it wears itself out. We need to 'give ourselves' to our tasks, too!" "Like a message that is written, read and erased, our troubles do pass eventually— they are erased." "Chalk has a single purpose—to communicate! So do we!"*

5) The trainer divides the participants into small groups of 6–8 people and gives a closed bag of objects to each group. Once everyone is settled, **Metaphors** worksheets are distributed and the trainer leads participants through the metaphor process. (5 minutes)

➤ Select a *current stressor* for which you want to generate a new viewpoint or additional coping options. Write this stressor at the top of your worksheet.

➤ Each person should take and object from the bag. Write your object in *Box A.*

➤ Use the process just demonstrated to identify the *FORM* and *FUNCTION* of your object and to *force fit* it onto your stressor as you search for creative options. Record your observations and ideas in *Boxes B, C* and *D* of your worksheet.

6) The trainer invites participants to practice using their immediate environment as a source of metaphors. (5 minutes)

➤ Glance around the room and select for your next focus some object that intrigues you. Write it in *Box E.*

➤ Then follow the same process as before. Identify the *FORM* and *FUNCTIONS*, then seek alternative perceptions and new creative coping strategies from the *force fit* process. Record your observations in *Boxes F, G* and *H* of the worksheet.

7) The trainer gives instructions for small group brainstorming. (2–3 minutes for each participant, about 15 minutes total)

➤ One-by-one share your insights with your small group. Each person should take 1 minute to share and then the group should take 1–2 minutes to generate "creative additions."

➤ Record additional coping ideas in *Boxes I* and *J* .

8) The trainer reconvenes the entire group and points out that common items for use as "force fit" metaphors are around us all the time waiting to spark our creativity and to enhance our coping capacity.

©1994 Whole Person Press 210 W Michigan Duluth MN 55802   (800) 247-6789

VARIATION

■ To reduce the time required, divide into 3–4 person groups for *Steps 5–7*. This may lower the creativity and energy level of participants.

TRAINER'S NOTES

METAPHORS

Please identify one stressor in your life that makes you fee "stuck in a rut," and for which you would like to discover some additional ideas for coping.

(the stressor I will focus on) _____

A. Object from the bag	C. FUNCTION How is it used? What does it do?	D. FORCE FIT How could I apply this to my stress?	I. BRAINSTORM Additional ideas from my group
B. FORM/Design What is it like? Characteristics?			
E. Object from the room	G. FUNCTION How is it used? What does it do?	H. FORCE FIT How could I apply this to my stress?	J. BRAINSTORM Additional ideas from my group
F. FORM/Design What is it like? Characteristics?			

86 S.O.S. FOR STRESS

Participants learn an over-arching paradigm for coping with stress and apply the specific strategies from this model to a personal stressor of their choice.

GOALS

To expand awareness of coping options.

To demonstrate the variety of coping approaches that could prove effective for any single stressor.

To encourage the use of under-utilized or neglected skills for managing stress.

GROUP SIZE

Unlimited.

TIME FRAME

30–50 minutes

MATERIALS

Blank paper for all participants.

PROCESS

1) The trainer introduces the exercise with a few brief comments on stress and coping which set the stage for the *SOS: Success Over Stress* coping paradigm.

   - The stress reaction is commonly fueled from two sources—the *external events* that impinge on our lives and our *internal reactions* to those events.

   - Since the source of stress is both *internal* (from within us) and *external* (provoked by our physical/interpersonal environment), the complete range of stress management strategies calls for us to alter our internal reactions as well as to control the external precipitators that initiate the stress cycle. When neither of these options proves particularly effective, we may activate a third strategy—gathering support from our environment.

2) The trainer distributes a sheet of paper to each participant. He asks everyone to choose a current stressor in their life that they would like

to cope with more effectively. Participants record their stressful situation in the upper left-hand corner.

☞ *For purposes of this exercise, participants should select a stressor of moderate to major impact in their lives. Minor stressors such as "an office mate who crunches apples too loudly," or "anger that I burned the eggs," are not recommended. Better to choose an issue of significance that could benefit from the concentrated attention it will receive during this exercise.*

3) The trainer explains that he will be presenting three different **SOS: Success Over Stress** strategies, describing several different coping skills and asking them to apply these alternative approaches to the stress that they have listed.

☞ *As you outline the points one at a time, suggest that people take notes on the strategies, using the left-hand side of the paper, and leaving room to answer the related coping application questions to the right.*

4) The trainer introduces **SOS** Strategy #1.

● **Start On (the) Situation.**

● Most people identify stress both with major life changes—such as divorce or a layoff—and with the myriad of tasks, demands, frustrations, conflicts, worries and hassles that plague them on a day-to-day basis. A primary approach to managing such stressful situations is to tackle them head on—to work at changing the external circumstance that is provoking the stress reaction.

The trainer describes several skills that are useful in working on the *external* source of stress and asks participants to reflect on how each approach might apply to their identified situation.

☞ *Be sure to expand the notes with additional details and your own examples so that the concepts come alive. Allow plenty of time for people to answer each "application" question.*

● **Set limits.** Establish priorities. Eliminate some activities. Simplify where possible. Schedule necessities. Refuse unreasonable demands. Choose your battles carefully.
  ➤ What limits do you need to set in order to cope more effectively? Make some notes for yourself.

● **Take charge.** Take responsibility for your predicament. Do something specific. Reduce uncertainty. Seek additional information. Face choices. Make decisions. Be assertive.

> ➤ In what ways could you take charge of your situation? What, specifically, do you need to do?

- **Minimize change.** Stay put. Keep to a schedule. Postpone decisions. Lay low. Cruise in neutral for awhile.

> ➤ How would minimizing change help you cope with your stressor? What changes can you postpone?

The trainer invites everyone to reflect on their applications of the *Start On (the) Situation* strategy, asking them to respond in writing to the following questions.

> ➤ What can you change about your current situation? How could you go about it?

5) The trainer presents the *SOS* Strategy #2.

- **Start On Self.**
- Stress never occurs without our "cooperation." Our response to stressors ultimately determines the level of stress we experience. Often we have more control over ourselves and our reactions than we do over the circumstances in which we find ourselves.

Participants are invited to consider several skills for altering their *internal* response. The trainer guides them in applying each approach to their stressor.

- **Take care of yourself.** Get adequate rest, slow down, try deep breathing, relax regularly, develop present-awareness, establish a daily routine, find quiet time, watch your physical health.

> ➤ How would taking better care of yourself help with your stress? What do you need to do to take better care of yourself? Jot down your self-care ideas.

- **Get away from it all.** Change your environment. Find a new spot to think, work, play, live. Develop external interests. Give yourself rewarding breaks. Exercise regularly.

> ➤ How could you get away from your stressor for awhile?

- **Strengthen your resistance.** Use antidotes to stress. Learn to tolerate uncertainty. Identify your wants and preferences and learn to satisfy them. Revise your unspoken rules and negative self-messages.

> ➤ How could strengthening your resistance help you cope with your stress?

- **Get your mental house in order.** Anticipate change. Develop your skills and competencies. Resolve your conflicts. Clarify your values. Focus your attention on what really counts.

> ➤ What would a clearer, stronger mind do to help you cope? How could you move in this direction?

The trainer asks participants to review their responses to the *Start On Self* Strategy and summarize in writing their answers to the questions below.

> ➤ Overall, what do you need to start doing to better care for yourself? What difference would this make for you in handling your stress?

6) The trainer describes the final *SOS* strategy.

● **Search Out Support.**

● Even if we have tried to change the situations and we've already done as much as we can to take care of ourself and go it alone, there's still more we can do. Our environment is chock full of resources (friends, experts, rituals, connections) that can support us during times of stress—if we only seek them out and take advantage of their strength.

The trainer outlines several networking approaches that might be effective in managing stress and invites participants to apply them in their own situations.

● **Utilize your environment.** Reach out for resources. Work within your context. Take advantage of your surroundings. Let your space protect and comfort you. Search out beauty.

> ➤ What resources in your environment have you neglected? How could tapping into the support of your environment help with your stress?

● **Share your burden.** Lean on someone you trust. Talk it out. Ask for help. Accept the comfort and encouragement of friends. Find a support group.

> ➤ Who could share your burden? How could that support help you with your stress?

● **Call out the horses.** Connect with the experts. Seek counsel and advice from professional resources in your community or workplace.

> ➤ What expertise could you call on in dealing with your particular stress? What stops you from asking for help?

● **Don't suffer on the sidelines.** Create support systems where they don't exist. Participate in ritual. Share others' experience. Support someone else. Make connections.

> ➤ How would getting involved again help you cope with your stress? What should you "jump into?"

©1994 Whole Person Press 210 W Michigan Duluth MN 55802   (800) 247-6789

The trainer invites participants to review their networking strategies in response to the following questions.

> ➤ What resources around you can you call on for support? How would it help you to do so?

7) The trainer suggests that the three SOS strategies, no matter how brilliantly outlined, will not be effective unless we are ready to *get going!*

The trainer challenges participants to apply what they have learned in this exercise about coping by making a plan and preparing to take some action. He guides them through the process.

> ➤ Look over all your comments on each separate coping skill, as well as the three major SOS strategies. Which SOS strategy shows the promise for your situation?

> ➤ What, specifically, should you/will you do first?

> ➤ What's your next step in coping?

> ➤ What must you do now to improve your coping style?

8) The trainer asks for a general sharing of insights and observations gained by participants during the process of this exercise.

VARIATIONS

■ If time permits the trainer may divide participants into small discussion groups for sharing of insights and action plans as part of *Step 8.*

■ The trainer could provide a worksheet that outlines the *SOS* strategies and specific skills in each. Participants mark their worksheets rather than taking notes. The convenience to participants may be offset by their tendency to "race through" the separate skills without carefully considering each one on its own merit.

The skills outlined in this exercise are adapted from James Mills, **Coping with Stress** *(New York: John Wiley & Sons, 1982).*

87 STRESS CLUSTERS

In this thought-provoking card game, participants utilize separate decks of stressor cards and coping cards to create stress scenarios and strategies for coping based on "the luck of the draw."

GOALS

To explore the stress generated by clusters of change.

To apply specific coping skills to a life-like stress scenario.

To promote problem-solving approaches to coping with stress.

TIME FRAME

40–60 minutes

GROUP SIZE

The exercise is described for 18–24 people but can easily be adapted for larger or smaller groups by adjusting the size and number of work teams. It is essential to have at least three teams, but they could range in size from three to eight participants.

MATERIALS

One **Stress Scenario** worksheet for each team (6–8 participants); one complete deck of **PILEUP** cards for every three teams (18–24 people total). The **PILEUP** card game is available from Whole Person Press.

This process works best when each team of participants can gather around a table to work together.

PROCESS

 Before beginning this exercise the trainer should familiarize herself with the PILEUP cards and separate each deck into three piles: 1) the yellow "stressor" cards; 2) the red and green "coper" cards; and 3) the rainbow "creative" cards. Each pile should be shuffled thoroughly.

A. Introductions and Team-Building (5–10 minutes)

1) The trainer briefly describes the process of the exercise, noting that teams will create a profile of a hypothetical person under stress who has experienced a random cluster of life events, much like we are often dealt in life. Teams will then exchange scenarios and develop creative coping strategies to deal with the clusters of change.

2) The trainer divides participants into at least three teams of 6–8 people each.

   ☞ *To randomize the group composition divide according to vowels in participants' first names. If some groups are too large, split them up by some other alphabetical criteria. If some groups are too small, instruct "leftovers" from one vowel team to join those of another, so that there are at least 3 teams and each of them has 6–8 members.*

3) Once all the teams have assembled and found a workspace in the room, the trainer directs team members to introduce themselves to each other and then select a team name (eg, "Stress Busters," "The A Team," "Coping Clowns," etc) and appoint a team recorder. (3–5 minutes)

   ☞ *While teams are getting acquainted, go around from team to team, giving each group a pile of yellow* **stressor** *cards equal to the number of people on the team. These should be placed face down on the table along with one* **Stress Clusters Clinic** *worksheet and an admonition not to "peek" until you give the word.*

B. Stress Clusters Scenarios (10–15 minutes)

4) The trainer calls time and gives instructions for the *Stress Clusters* process.

   ➤ Decide who will go first. The first person should draw one card from the stress PILEUP.

   ➤ Read the information on your card out loud. Every card describes one or two life events that can cause stress or strain. After you read the stressors on your card, place it face up on the table and invite the group to choose one event from your card that will be added to your team's *stress cluster.*

   ➤ The recorder should write down the selected stressor in *Section A* of the worksheet.

➤ Go around the group repeating this process until all the cards have been read and the chosen stressors recorded on your team's worksheet.

☞ *When the majority of groups are nearly finished, interrupt with the final instruction.*

➤ When you have finished choosing your stresses and strains, stop and look over your team's *pileup* of stressors. Talk together about what other changes would probably accompany this particular *stress cluster*. For example, if your *pileup* includes *move to a new city*, it's likely that other changes—such as *new home, change in schools, new friendship patterns*, etc—would also occur.

➤ The recorder should add these associated stressors to the team list.

5) After 3–5 minutes the trainer interrupts with directions for composing *stress scenarios.*

➤ As a team, look over your list of stressors and make up a story about a hypothetical person who has experienced the entire cluster of life change events represented by your team's *stress pileup*. Imagine as many specific details as you can and make the story as true to life as possible.

☞ *To demonstrate this process, make up your own sample scenario from a random deal of stressors and tell it to the group, or use this example:*

PILEUP stressor cards you are dealt: death of a family member, loss of job, increased hassles with the kids over use of the car, Christmas, troubles with the boss, increased alcohol consumption.

Sample scenario: Tom's mother died six weeks ago after a long illness that had depleted the family bank account and sapped their emotional and physical energy. Jan, Tom's wife, quit her job to help care for his mom—which has meant they got behind on car payments. Tom's boss is giving him trouble for taking time off and not being available for weekend work. He's started drinking regularly to unwind at the end of the day. All of Tom's siblings came for Christmas, since they knew it would be Mom's last. It was an exhausting holiday, with lots of intense conversations and late evenings as well as arguments about putting Mom in a home. Tom and Jan are concerned about 16-year-old Jason's group of friends and their Friday night hot-rodding. So far they've refused Jason's requests for the car on weekends, but he is bugging them for more driving privileges.

➤ Take 5 minutes to brainstorm and 4–5 minutes to polish your final story. The recorder should note all the ideas generated. Once the team has decided on the final details of the scenario, the recorder should write it down in *Section B* of the worksheet. Write legibly and in narrative style so that the next team will be able to read your story easily.

☞ *As the teams are finishing up their scenarios, circulate and give each group a pack of coping cards equal in number to the team members, place them face down in a stack on the table.*

Announce "one minute to finish up," and then wait a moment or two before proceeding to the next step.

C. Applying Coping Strategies (10–15 minutes)

6) The trainer asks recorders to "dump" their completed *stress scenario* on the neighboring team (clockwise), who will be challenged to cope with it.

➤ In each team, one person should read to the other team members the *scenario* you have just received.

7) When all the teams are done, the trainer gives instructions for developing *coping plans.*

➤ The new pile of cards on your table represents the coping resources available to the hypothetical person in the scenario you just read. Some are *positive copers* (GREEN cards) that are often effective for dealing with stress. And some are *negative* or *questionable copers* (RED cards) that may temporarily relieve stress, but have undesirable side effects.

➤ Each person should take a turn. Draw a coping card from the pile and read the information, including the skill name and the examples of how it might be used.

➤ Place the card face up on the table. The recorder should write the coper in *Section D* of the worksheet. Your team should spend a minute or two brainstorming ideas about how this particular coping strategy could prove useful in managing the stress of this scenario.

➤ Repeat this process for each person and their coping card.

©1994 Whole Person Press 210 W Michigan Duluth MN 55802   (800) 247-6789

☞ *Encourage groups to explore potential positive and negative results of using the RED **negative** copers and the many alternative options for activating each of the GREEN **positive** copers.*

8) After 8–10 minutes the trainer interrupts the process and directs each group to incorporate the multitude of coping ideas they have generated into a **comprehensive management plan** for dealing with the stress scenario that was dumped on them. The recorders should write down the details of the coping plan in **Section C** of the worksheet. (5 minutes)

☞ *While groups are finishing up, go around and deal each team 2 **rainbow** cards, face down on the table.*

D. Wild Cards: Creative Problem Solving (8–10 min)

9) Once again the trainer instructs each team to pass on their **stress scenario** worksheet (complete with **coping plan**) to the neighboring team (clockwise). In each team one person reads both the stress scenario written by the original group and the coping strategy developed by the second team.

10) When the teams are finished reading, the trainer announces the **creative twist**. (5–8 minutes)

➤ The final two cards are **wild cards**—designed to help stretch your imagination and stimulate creative approaches to coping.

➤ Read the RAINBOW **wild cards** you were dealt and use the creative problem solving questions listed on each to embellish the coping scenario you received.

➤ Be as creative and "off-the-wall" as possible in suggesting whatever outrageous possibilities come to mind. Work quickly and try to keep a steady stream of ideas flowing as rapidly as possible.

➤ Recorders should write your team's cards in **Box E** of the worksheet and in **Box F** summarize all the unusual applications and creative twists generated by your group.

E. Team Reports and Wrap-Up (8–10 minutes)

11) The trainer reconvenes the entire group and asks the team recorders, one-by-one, to read their worksheets, including the stress scenario written by the first group, the coping strategies suggested by the second

group, and selected highlights from the creative twists added by their own team. (6–10 minutes)

12) In closing, the trainer may solicit from participants their insights and observations about stress clusters, creative coping strategies and the process of this exercise.

VARIATIONS

■ The yellow stressor cards include numbers (representing research data on the relative amount of stress caused by each change) and symbols signifying the category of the stressor (eg, family strain, financial, transitions, etc). As part of *Step 4* teams could analyze the types and severity of their stress cluster and compare that distribution with other teams.

■ The coping cards are divided into six categories of positive skills (physical, mental, spiritual, family, interpersonal and diversion), as well as 14 negative coping activities. As part of *Step 8* teams could analyze the various types of coping strategies represented by the cards they have drawn and discuss the importance of cultivating a wide variety of coping alternatives.

TRAINER'S NOTES

STRESS CLUSTERS CLINIC

A. STRESSORS we drew	B. STRESS SCENARIO
	Here's the person and the situation:

C. COPING STRATEGY	D. COPING cards we drew
Here's how we suggest handling it:	

E. RAINBOW cards we drew	F. CREATIVE TWISTS we recommend

88 CORPORATE PRESENTATION

In this affirming small group activity, participants give themselves a lecture about the ten best methods for managing stress.

GOALS

To tap into participants' wisdom about coping with stress.

To provide an overview of stress management strategies.

GROUP SIZE

Described for 30–60 people, but works well with smaller groups, too.

TIME FRAME

20–30 minutes

MATERIALS

Newsprint and markers for each small group; flip chart or blackboard for the trainer.

PROCESS

1) The trainer introduces the goals and process of the exercise.

   ● During the next half hour we will be searching for a wide spectrum of coping strategies that might be helpful in managing stress.

   ● Everyone is an expert on coping—We all successfully manage a steady stream of potential stressors day by day across our lifetime. In this exercise we will create a corporate presentation based on the collected wisdom of the group.

2) The trainer designates 10 different spots in the room, assigns each location a numeral (0 to 9), and then gives instructions for creating small groups.

   ➤ Take out a dollar bill (a five or ten will do)—or borrow one from a neighbor.

   ➤ Look at the bill and notice the *last digit* of the serial number. Go to the appointed area in the room that matches your digit.

   👉 *This should create small groups of 3–6 people. The groups can be uneven, but if necessary, combine groups, so that none has fewer than 3 or 4 members. With less than 30 people, decide how many groups (4 to 6 people each) are needed and then divide by combining last digits. For two groups, separate by odd and even serial numbers. For five groups, divide in (0–1, 2–3, etc). Or use some other method to form small groups.*

3) Once all the groups are settled, the trainer outlines the challenge.

> ➤ Spend 15 minutes as a group giving yourselves a lecture on the topic: ***The ten best strategies for coping with stress.***

> ➤ Draw out the wisdom of your group. Make sure that everyone has input.

> ➤ Record all your ideas on newsprint.

4) After 15 minutes the trainer interrupts.

> ➤ Spend the next 5 minutes looking over your list and determining which coping methods you think are most effective in dealing with stress.

5) The trainer reconvenes the entire group and announces that it's now time for the ***corporate presentation***. Participants are invited to share their answers to the question, "What are the ten best strategies for coping with stress?"

> ☞ *Encourage participants to "build a case" for the potency and value of the copers they suggest. Offer to help with the presentation by adding a few ideas along the way.*

As people volunteer their insights, the trainer records the ideas on the board, expanding, amplifying, connecting, integrating, challenging where appropriate—and for each contribution, thanks the presenter.

> ☞ *If participants seem reluctant to speak up, try a little contest between groups or offer a reward for everyone who contributes.*

6) The trainer builds on the data base generated by the group to present his own schema of the most effective strategies for managing stress.

VARIATION

> ■ If time permits before *Step 6*, instruct the group to reach a consensus on the ten best coping ideas suggested. Then facilitate an energetic discussion around this issue.

Submitted by Joel Goodman.

©1994 Whole Person Press 210 W Michigan Duluth MN 55802   (800) 247-6789

89 IMAGINE SUCCESS

Participants practice the technique of positive visualization, imagining themselves as successfully employing a selected coping skill.

GOALS

To increase the probability of successful stress management through the use of positive visualization.

To apply a practical principle of stress management within the learning experience.

GROUP SIZE

Unlimited; also effective for use with individuals.

TIME FRAME

15–30 minutes

PROCESS

☞ *This exercise most appropriately follows a presentation in which participants have examined the multitude of positive coping strategies available to them.*

1) The trainer asks participants to reflect on their life stress and how they would like to cope differently.

☞ *Give a few examples (ideally drawn from previous discussion in the group) before asking participants to write down the single stressor and specific coping they have selected.*

➤ Identify one stressor you would particularly like to manage better.

➤ Choose one strategy you've learned about here that you imagine might be effective in coping with that stressor.

2) The trainer prepares the group by briefly describing the exercise and "walking through" the steps of the positive visualization process, answering any questions that may arise.

She then provides a theoretical framework for "imagining success."

● Behavioral theory postulates that if we can imagine ourselves successfully changing our behavior, we are more likely to follow through on that new behavior in our everyday life. The positive visualization you will experience in this exercise is a process of "thinking" your way into new ways of acting and being.

● **Imaging is more powerful than will power.** If you first imagine yourself experiencing success with a new skill, you are far more likely, in fact, to be successful when you put that skill into practice.

● World-class athletes in every sport use positive visualization to improve their concentration and performance. The same process will work for you if you want to improve your record as a stress manager!

3) The trainer asks people to get comfortable in their chairs, or to move around the room and find a place where they can relax fully. She invites them to loosen any tight clothing such as ties, belts, etc.

☞ *Pause to allow time for this position change and "settling in."*

4) As soon as everyone is settled, the trainer guides participants through the positive visualization process, using statements and questions similar to those included in the **Imagine Success** script below. (5–8 minutes)

5) After people have completed the visualization, the trainer divides participants into triads to share their experiences with each other. (8–15 minutes)

➤ Describe your visualization as if you are retelling a dream—slowly drawing the scene, then embellishing it with the feelings you experienced.

➤ Concentrate on how you successfully coped with your stress by using your selected coping skills.

☞ *It is important to acknowledge that some people may have had difficulty imagining the scene and their success with stress. Emphasize that visualization is also a skill that becomes easier with practice. Encourage people to try again with another coping skill—some strategies may work better than others in real life—and in visualization! Reassure people who "didn't quite get into this" so that they don't feel like failures! This exercise is designed to help people feel* **successful***!*

VARIATIONS

■ During or after *Step 5* invite participants—either in triads or as a large group—to share the coping skill they selected and to articulate the positive change they imagine will happen in their lives as they begin to utilize this skill more fully.

■ To close the exercise, participants write a set of recommendations for themselves, based on their visualization experience. This could take the form of a behavioral contract or an inspirational letter to be mailed to themselves at the end of the learning experience.

TRAINER'S NOTES

IMAGINE SUCCESS Script

Close your eyes . . . take some deep breaths . . .
Tune out the noises and the people around you . . . focus on yourself.
> ☞ *Pause and model these instructions by taking several*
> *deep breaths yourself, sighing and slowing your voice.*

Now I'd like you to think about the stressor you selected as your focus . . .
Recall it . . . Bring it to life right now . . .

> *Say to yourself, "I feel very stressed*
> *when   (insert your stressor)   happens in my life . . . "*
>
> > *Pause*

> *Imagine how your whole self responds to this stress.*
> *Feel all your stress symptoms . . .*
>
> > *Pause*

> *Allow yourself to imagine all the pain that stress brings you . . .*
>
> > *Pause*

*Now recall the **coping skill** you selected . . . Imagine how this skill can*
help you deal creatively with the stressor.

> > *Pause*

> *Say to yourself, "When I feel stressed, I will successfully*
> *use   (insert your skill)   to relieve and cope with my stress.*
> *It will help me a great deal . . . "*
>
> > *Pause*

> *Imagine yourself practicing this skill.*
> *Actually envision how you look . . . how your body feels . . .*
> *and exactly how you act out this skill . . .*
>
> > *Pause*

> > *What are you doing? . . . How does it feel? . . .*
> > *How do you feel? . . .*
> >
> > > *Pause*

> > *How does your body feel? . . .*
> >
> > > *Pause*

©1994 Whole Person Press 210 W Michigan Duluth MN 55802   (800) 247-6789

Imagine yourself successfully coping with your stress . . .
using this skill . . .
Watch yourself dealing with your stress . . .

Pause

What happens to your stress? . . .

Pause

Observe the positive effects that extend to other areas of your life . . .

Pause

Imagine yourself successfully coping with your stress . . .

Pause

Feel the relief and positive energy that flows through you as you become aware of your ability to cope and to feel better . . .

Pause

Hold on to your good feelings . . .
Be confident that you can, in fact, take charge of the stress in your life . . .

Pause

Now, begin preparing yourself to end this exercise . . .
Come back into an awareness of the room where you are now.

Pause

Slowly move a few muscles, stretch and take another deep breath . . .

Pause

Then slowly open your eyes and begin to notice your surroundings . . .

Pause

☞ *Repeat this last set of instructions as necessary until all have "come back into the room."*

Skill Builders

90 CONFLICT MANAGEMENT

In this thought-provoking learning experience participants explore four conflict-prevention skills and experiment with applying them to specific conflict situations.

GOALS

To identify conflict situations that cause stress.

To discover and practice alternative approaches for preventing or managing conflict.

GROUP SIZE

Unlimited.

TIME FRAME

60 minutes

MATERIALS

Conflict Alternatives worksheets for all participants; blackboard or flip chart.

PROCESS

1) The trainer begins by asking participants for examples of conflict and typical conflict situations that they experience (eg, misunderstanding, personality clash, poor performance, difference of opinion or values, lack of cooperation, authority issues, differing goals, competition, etc). As examples are suggested, the trainer records them on the board.

2) After a lengthy and comprehensive list of conflicts has been generated, the trainer introduces the concept of conflict management and describes what participants can expect from this session. Some or all of the following points could be included:

   ● It's not what you know, but what you do with what you know that counts in conflict management.

   ● This session doesn't promise that you will be able to **control** conflicts in your life—after all, people are unpredictable. Nor will taking this course assure that you will win in all conflict situations.

- Managing conflict does not guarantee the outcome, but it may take away the power of the other person or the situation to stress you.
- Most of our attitudes toward conflict are shaped early in life by messages we learn from our environment—eg, "Button your lip!" "Turn the other cheek!" "Fighting never solved anything!" etc. Most people learn to dislike, avoid, or clam up in conflict situations. We believe that it's wrong, or at least not "nice" to have conflicts.

3) The trainer goes on to offer an alternative understanding of the nature of conflict—that it is *natural, inevitable* and *desirable*—and challenges participants to begin changing their attitudes:

- Conflict is an *inevitable* part of life. It is inherent in our differentness— our varying motivations, backgrounds, perspectives, values, needs, goals, feelings, expectations, opinions.
- Conflict is *desirable* because opposition is a way to think through all the alternatives. Conflict is a valuable tool to make sure that all major aspects of important matters are carefully considered.
- Conflict becomes *stressful* when reality doesn't coincide with our expectations. If we "believe" (expect) that conflict is unnatural— then the reality of conflict is likely to be upsetting!
- To manage conflict successfully, we need to change our expectations. If we accept conflict as a natural part of life, we can free our energy to focus attention on how to *cope* with it.

4) The trainer distributes **Conflict Alternatives** and asks participants to reflect on conflict in their lives.

➤ List several conflict situations that you have experienced recently, including at least a few that were especially difficult or are still needing to be resolved.

➤ Write each conflict in a separate box at the left of the worksheet.

5) The trainer explains that the worksheet will be used during the remainder of the session to record insights as participants explore four conflict management strategies that are useful in a wide variety of settings.

- Cultivate a positive mental attitude.
- Focus on the issue, not the person.
- Increase your tolerance level.
- Keep conflict in perspective.

6) The trainer asks for volunteers to describe how they typically feel in conflict situations, such as being called on the carpet, a family argument or just disagreeing about what movie to attend.

After several people have given examples (eg, defensive, scared, anxious, angry, upset, etc) she notes that such negative feelings often accompany conflict situations, which is why the first conflict management skill, *Positive Mental Attitude* is so important.

- Often we perceive conflict as a challenge to our personal beliefs, opinions, actions, authority. Even when the conflict is minor we experience an implied criticism of our own position.

- We usually respond in one of two ways—we kick ourselves for being inadequate or we strike out to protect our position or self-esteem. Neither response helps resolve the conflict.

- To deal creatively with conflict, we need to feel powerful and competent. Instead of generating a stream of mental putdowns—such as "I failed again," or "I don't measure up," or "This is terrible," or "He's right and I'm wrong," or "It's awful to be caught," etc— we need to focus on positive messages such as, "My worth doesn't depend on being perfect," or "I can learn from this," or "This is upsetting, but I know how to deal with it," or "I have the same rights as others," or "I am valuable and capable," or "This could be hairy, but I believe in myself," etc.

7) The trainer invites participants to reflect on each of the conflict situations identified on their **Conflict Alternatives** worksheet and decide whether a more positive mental attitude would be helpful in managing that particular conflict.

➤ For each situation ask yourself:
>   What positive messages could I tell myself in the midst of this conflict that would help raise my self-esteem and therefore my capacity to resolve the conflict?

➤ Jot down your answers in the column labeled *Raise Self Esteem*.

8) After most participants have completed the self-esteem portion of the worksheet, the trainer outlines the second strategy for managing conflict: *Focus on the Issue, Not the Person.*

- Conflict is often attributed to negative personality characteristics or behaviors of people (eg, "I have a slave-driver for a boss," "She's a lazy typist," etc).

- In fact, most conflicts can be redefined as an issue resulting from circumstances that affect both parties. This opens the door to resolution because these circumstances can potentially be changed when both parties search together for a solution (eg, "The office is understaffed," "The workload is erratic," "We need to set priorities," etc).

- Although there are instances when a person's personality is the problem—and must be honestly dealt with—it is almost always more constructive to state the conflict as an *issue* and not attack or blame the *persons* involved.

9) The trainer asks for examples of conflict situations and demonstrates stating each conflict in both a ***person-focused*** and an ***issue-focused*** manner. After modeling one or two examples, she may ask the group to try redefining a few more conflicts as person and issue-focused.

10) Once the group seems to understand the process, the trainer helps participants articulate their potential use of this skill.

   ➤ Look again at your worksheets and apply the issue/person principle in each situation.

   ➤ For each conflict answer the question:

      ➤ How could focusing on the issue rather than the person be helpful in resolving or preventing this conflict?

   ➤ Write your responses in the column marked ***Focus On The Issue.***

11) After most people have finished recording their observations, the trainer invites participants to consider the third strategy for conflict management—***Heighten Your Tolerance Level***. She describes the rationale and process for implementing this approach:

   - In general most people have unrealistic expectations for other people. We expect them to act just the way we want them to, and we expect them to be perfect! How outrageous! People are human beings—not gods!

   - It is impossible to control other people—even though sometimes we would like to. People will be frustrating, difficult, angry, selfish, incompetent—no matter what we prefer. We can prevent or minimize the stress of conflict if we raise our tolerance level toward other people's behavior. How do we become more tolerant? The first step is to change the way we talk to ourselves.

● When faced with a conflict people tend to "awfulize" about the situation, saying things to themselves like, "I can't stand him another minute!" Well, you *can* stand him another minute . . . and you will! Such common self-talk is comical when actually spoken outloud.

12) The trainer solicits from participants examples of self-talk that reinforces our stance of intolerance (eg, "I'm going to die if this doesn't get decided soon!" "I hate working with her!" "He drives me crazy!"). For each negative statement the group is challenged to suggest more tolerant alternatives (eg, "This person's behavior is frustrating to me. However, I cannot expect her to be perfect—and she is not likely to change. I'd better accept it and go on," etc).

13) The trainer invites participants to apply the increased tolerance level strategy to their conflicts.

➤ Look over your list of conflicts. In the column marked *Increased Tolerance* for each conflict, write your answers to these four questions.

➣ How might this situation benefit from increased tolerance on my part?

➣ What unrealistic expectations do I have here?

➣ What intolerant messages am I telling myself?

➣ What more tolerant messages could I use instead?

14) The trainer invites participants to consider the final strategy for managing conflict—*Keeping It In Perspective.*

➤ Pretend that you have just been awarded $25. This sum represents the total investment of energy and stress you are currently making in the conflicts listed on your worksheet.

➤ Distribute the $25 among the conflicts according how much energy or worry you are spending (or usually spend) on each one. Record the amounts in the *Perspective* column of your worksheet.

☞ *Pause long enough for everyone to spend their $25.*

➤ Now review your list of conflicts again and *reallocate* the money, this time based on how much each conflict is *really worth*. What is its true value and importance in the long run?

15) The trainer solicits insights and reactions from the group, prompting them with questions like these.

✔ Where are you spending the most? Is the conflict worth it?

✔ What is the relationship between your expenditure and the importance of the conflict?

16) The trainer concludes by citing the "Law of Creeping Importance":

● If you rate the importance of conflicts on a scale of 1 to 10, **all
conflicts will creep up to become 10s.** The only counterbalance to
this law is to be vigilant about keeping conflicts in perspective.

17) The trainer invites participants to practice a conflict management skill.

➤ Look over your worksheet and choose one conflict situation you
would like to work on—and one of the four management skill/
strategies you would like to practice applying to that situation.

➤ Pair up with a neighbor and take turns role playing your conflict
situation, experimenting with the new skill.

☞ *Adjust the structure, style and length of the role play to your
group. One person begins by explaining his conflict situation
and describing the skill he wants to try. His partner can take
either role in the conflict. The pairs role play the situation for
2–3 minutes or until the original person is satisfied. He then
notes any good ideas generated during the role play before
going on to practice the other person's situation.*

18) The trainer reconvenes the large group and asks for insights and
observations on any aspect of conflict management. In conclusion, she
summarizes the key points from the session and encourages participants to continue experimenting with these four strategies in a variety
of conflict situations.

VARIATIONS

■ The icebreaker, **Models** (p 1), could be adapted for conflict management and included as part of *Step 1*.

■ *Step 5* could be spiced up by adding the irrational beliefs **Boo-Down**
(**Stress 1**, p 113).

■ If time permits, the role plays in *Step 17* could be expanded by having
partners practice all four management strategies.

Submitted by Pat Miller.

Conflict Situations	Raise Self-Esteem	Stay Issue-Centered	Increase Tolerance	Keep In Perspective

CONFLICT MANAGEMENT

91 EIGHT-MINUTE STRESS BREAK

Participants learn a 15-step stretch routine that can be used as a stress break any time of the day.

GOALS

To demonstrate the effectiveness of exercise as a stress management technique.

To stretch all the major muscle groups.

GROUP SIZE

Unlimited, as long as there is sufficient space for everyone to move freely.

TIME FRAME

10 minutes

MATERIALS

Tape recorder and peppy music.

PROCESS

1) The trainer briefly describes typical benefits of stretching and exercise as stress management techniques:

   ● Stretching and vigorous exercise both help discharge accumulated physical tension from the various muscle groups.

   ● The increased flow of blood and oxygen to the muscles usually stimulates an increased energy level.

   ● Both types of physical activity provide a distraction from emotional or mental strain.

   ● Stretching and exercise are effective *preventive* measures for dealing with stress by systematically letting go of tension before it accumulates to unhealthy proportions. These techniques also are effective *in crisis situations* to relieve the physical effects of stress.

2) The trainer turns on the music and participants join in as he demonstrates the **Eight-Minute Stress Break** routine which can easily be incorporated into a busy schedule.

VARIATIONS

■ Choose only a few exercises to teach during this presentation (eg, all upper body stretches). Then sprinkle the other routines throughout the remainder of the session.

■ To model how this skill could be used in real life, teach the whole sequence at once and then sprinkle repeat performances as mini stretch breaks during unexpected or particularly stressful moments in the remainder of the learning experience.

■ If the course is several sessions long, go through the sequence once at every meeting in order to entrench the routine in participants' minds.

■ After *Step 2* hand out a list of the 14 stretches. Ask people to identify their favorites and make a list of those they especially want to use in the future and the situations where they most need to!

TRAINER'S NOTES

Submitted by Keith Sehnert, MD, author of **The Family Doctor's Health Tips** *(Meadowbrook, 1981), from which this exercise is adapted.*

EIGHT-MINUTE STRESS BREAK

1. The 360 Stretch.
Begin with your body relaxed, arms and hands loose at your sides. Pull your right shoulder up and with one smooth movement, bring the shoulder back and around, making a complete circle. Repeat this same circular motion with the left shoulder.
Continue stretching one shoulder, then the other, 5 times each. Then reverse the direction, using alternate shoulders, 5 times each. This should loosen up your neck, back and shoulders—places where most people store tension.

2. Starfish Stretch.
Begin with your arms stretched overhead, slightly bent, eyes turned upward.
In a single motion, open your hands, spread your fingers wide, and reach up as high as you can. Hold that position for a few seconds. Then close your fists and lower your arms, with elbows bent. Rest a few seconds and then repeat the starfish stretch/rest sequence 10–15 times.
For variety, stretch to the side.

3. Snow Angels.
Allow your arms to hang loose at your sides. Begin to loosen your wrists by shaking your hands, allowing them to flop as freely as possible.
Continue to shake and flop as you slowly raise your arms to the side and up until your hands touch overhead. Then allow your arms to gradually drop, still shaking and loosening the wrists.

4. Tall Grass Stalk.
Extend your arms out in front of you. While concentrating on your shoulders, slowly sweep your hands and arms to the side and back, as if pushing tall grass out of the way.
You should feel a pull along your shoulders and arms.
Stretch your arms out again and "stalk" for 10 more steps.

5. Bunny Hop.
Put your hands on your hips and hop twice on your right foot. Now hop twice on your left foot. Continue these double hops, alternating feet and adding a side kick or a cross kick on the second hop. Continue hopping and kicking for 30 seconds, varying your tempo and kick height.

6. Hoe-Down.
Start by getting centered, feet firmly planted, knees slightly bent.
Lift your right knee up towards your chest, slap it with your left hand and then lower your leg and stretch it to the side, toes pointing outward. Repeat the hoe-down lift 3 more times and then try the left leg for 4 counts.

7. Cloud Walk.
This is a slow step, rolling from heel to toe, one foot at a time, gently stretching the legs and feet. Your whole body should be relaxed.
Pick up the tempo of the heel-toe roll until you reach a slow jog, raising your feet slightly off the floor at each step. Continue at this pace for 30 seconds.

8. Dippity-Do.
Start with your legs slightly apart. Dip your body into an easy kneebend and then spring back to the upright position.
Continue to bend and spring back for 30 seconds, adding rhythmic arm swings as you increase your pace.

©1994 Whole Person Press 210 W Michigan Duluth MN 55802   (800) 247-6789

EIGHT-MINUTE STRESS BREAK (cont)

9. Arch Stretch.
With knees slightly bent, join your hands comfortably behind your back.
Slowly arch your back, letting your hands and stiff arms pull your shoulders and head down toward the floor.
Hold for 5 counts and then relax, allowing your head to fall forward and your shoulders to curl toward the front.
Repeat 7 times.

10. Twister.
With feet shoulder width apart and knees bent, put your hands on your hips.
Keep your back straight as you twist your shoulders and trunk to the right 3 times and then return to face forward. Now twist to the opposite side for 3 counts and return to the center.
Continue to twist for 8 sets.

11. Body Bounce.
With feet apart, arms at your sides, bend sideways at the waist, stretching your hand down your leg as you straighten up. Repeat the stretch and bounce to the other side. Do 5 body bounces on each side.
Now add your arms to the stretching movement. With your left arm, reach up and over as you bounce to the left 3 counts.
Do 5 sets on each side.

12. Sneak Peek.
Stand straight with your neck, shoulders and back as relaxed as possible.
Tilt your head to the left. Now slowly roll your head so that your chin falls to your chest and then comes up as your head tilts to the right. Now look back over your right shoulder, hold the pose and then relax.
Repeat the stretch, this time starting with your head tilted to the right and ending with a sneak peek over your left shoulder.
Do four peeks on each side.

13. The Wave.
Stand straight with your arms at your sides, palms facing out.
As you take a long deep breath, slowly (4 counts) raise your arms up over your head. Now, as you exhale slowly, bring your arms back down, palms facing downward (4 counts).
Repeat this languid wave 6 times.

14. Hang Loose.
Time to shake out your body.
Flap your arms, twist your wrists, shrug your shoulders, jiggle your legs, shake your feet, flex your knees.
Bounce your booty until your whole body feels tingly, loose and relaxed.

92 STOP LOOK AND LISTEN

Using a do-it-yourself study guide, trios of participants experiment with techniques to improve listening skills and explore applications of empathy as a stress management strategy.

GOALS

To explore the value of listening as a coping skill in stressful situations.

To practice listening skills.

GROUP SIZE

Works best with 15 or more people, if there is plenty of space for small groups to meet separately.

TIME FRAME

60 minutes

MATERIALS

Newsprint easel or blackboard; **Stop, Look and Listen** flip guides for each participant (to be photocopied, cut, assembled and stapled before the meeting).

PROCESS

☞ *The energizer* **You're Not Listening** *(p 129) makes an excellent introduction to this exercise.*

The unusual feature of this listening exercise is the self-directed booklet that triads of participants use to work their way through the process. After your introductory chalktalk, all you as a trainer need to do is turn people loose, keep time, periodically announce when to move to the next page, and then sit back and see what happens!

1) The trainer introduces the exercise by announcing that the next hour or so will be spent in developing an unusual but powerful coping skill—listening.

She asks the group for ideas on why listening might be a useful skill for managing stress, and lists the suggestions on the blackboard or newsprint. As people contribute, she weaves their responses into a brief chalktalk on communication, stress and listening:

- Most people are good listeners when they want to be, but many simply don't choose to use this skill as frequently as they might—especially in stressful situations.

- **Breakdowns in our communication is a common cause of stress.** Misunderstanding, misinterpretation, hidden agendas, unresolved conflicts and disagreements may trigger our stress response.

- One way to handle such breakdowns and unstress ourselves in the process is to **respond with empathy** rather than anger or defensiveness. This response forces us to acknowledge the other person's point of view which broadens our perspective at the same time it affirms the other's experience.

2) The trainer briefly describes empathy and the **Stop, Look and Listen** paradigm.

- Empathy is a special kind of listening that literally means to "feel in," or to stand in another's shoes for a moment—to get inside that person's experience, to soak it up, and try to view it from his or her perspective.

- This is not a passive process. Being a good listener means more than just allowing the other person to talk—although that's a good start. Empathy involves a three-step process—**Stop, Look and Listen.**
  - **Stop.** Stop competing for attention. Stop worrying about your own feelings. Be quiet. Put aside your judgments and expectations about the person or the topic. Try to approach this with an open mind. Stop and take a deep breath. As you exhale, let go of your own agenda. Choose to focus on the other person.
  - **Look.** Look at the other person, eyeball to eyeball. Pay attention and show your interest. Get involved. Notice verbals and non-verbals. Observe, but don't interpret. Explore, don't judge. Look for this person's unique viewpoint. Put on his or her glasses and look at the world through those lenses.
  - **Listen.** Listen to what the person says. Listen to the words and the body language. Listen to the meanings behind the message. Listen to the feelings. Listen to the silence and reflect on what you've heard. Now respond—let the other person know what you've heard. Paraphrase. Comment on what you noticed—without interpreting. Feed back your perceptions and check them out (eg,"Is this what you meant? thought? felt?"). If you've misunderstood, reach out and try again to understand.

3) The trainer divides participants into groups of three people each, and instructs them to decide—for the purpose of this exercise—who will be "A," who will be "B," and who will be "C."

While groups are deciding, she distributes a copy of the **Stop, Look and Listen** flip guide to all participants, requesting that they not look at the booklet until directed.

4) The trainer outlines the process of the exercise:

> ➤ Most of the remaining time will be spent in your trios, completing the process described in this do-it-yourself flip guide. You will practice the skill of listening to each other by dialoguing about various topics assigned by the flip guides.

> ➤ In most of the 5–10 minute segments, two people in the trio will dialogue while the other remains silent—observing the listening process. These roles switch for each segment.

> ➤ The flip guide gives complete instructions, including questions to be discussed and roles to be taken by each person. When there is more than one question on a page, the two people "in dialogue" take turns listening to each other's answers to one question before moving on to the next.

> ➤ While dialoguing, you are to listen intently to each other and try to fully understand what the other is saying. This will take time—and you may not be able to answer all the questions in the time allotted. That's great! The purpose is to *listen* to each other, not to race through to the end!

> ➤ I will keep time. Follow the instructions in the booklet and unless it specifically says to turn to the next page, wait for my signal before moving on.

5) The trainer instructs participants to introduce themselves and look at the first three pages of the flip guide, which are a self-paced introduction. She reminds everyone to follow the directions in the guide and that she will keep track of time and announce when to move on. (5–6 minutes)

☞ *You may want to use a bell, harmonica or whistle to indicate the time. Be sure you are familiar with the timetable and instructions on each flip guide page so that you can keep time correctly and answer any questions. When you announce the time, remind people to use their empathic skills (eg, "Remember to paraphrase and check out your perceptions!" or "Take your time— listen with empathy!" etc.)*

6) When the last page is finished, the trainer asks the sextets to spend 3 more minutes brainstorming a list of stressful situations where empathy would be an effective stress management strategy.

7) The trainer reconvenes the entire group and asks for insights and observations about the experience of listening and the value of listening as a coping skill. After several people have shared, she solicits examples of situations where the skill might be useful, listing them on the board and using the data generated to summarize learnings from the session.

8) In closing, the trainer issues a final challenge:
- I can teach you the skill of listening, but I can't decide for you when you will use it. It's your choice when you implement it. Practice it so you'll be ready! Then choose to use it in some unlikely situations—and see what happens!

VARIATIONS

■ If time is limited, some of the listening processes from the flip guides may be shortened or skipped entirely. Be aware, however, that when the process is shortened the intensity and benefit of the experience will also be lessened.

TRAINER'S NOTES

STOP, LOOK AND LISTEN
dialogue instructions

1

Read this section silently. Do not look ahead in this booklet.

When we're under pressure, one of the first things that is likely to buckle is our ability to listen. Too bad! Empathy—the process of active, care-full listening—is one of the best stress management techniques available.

This exercise is designed to help you and your partners explore the value of listening when under stress. So, during the next hour, give yourself permission to STOP, LOOK and LISTEN.

STOP   Take a deep breath, exhale, and get ready to pay attention.

LOOK   Put on your partner's perceptual glasses and try to see his or her viewpoint rather than concentrating on your own.

LISTEN Tune in to the meaning behind the words, the person behind the pitter-patter.

Go on to the next page.

2

All information shared here is strictly confidential!

You will be engaging in a series of conversations, alternating roles as **observer**, **sharer**, and **listener**. Follow the instructions and take turns as indicated—both partners respond to each question before moving on.

When it is your turn to speak, respond to the questions at whatever level of disclosure feels comfortable. You may also decline to answer any question.

When you are listening, be sure to practice all the empathic listening skills.
   SHOW INTEREST: with eye contact, nods, "uh-huhs."
   REACH OUT: to pick up on both the verbal and non-verbal message.
   FOCUS ON YOUR PARTNER: set aside your own agenda.
   RESPOND: summarize periodically, check your perceptions.

When you are observing, pay attention to the process and impact of listening. At the end of the hour you will have a chance to share your insights.

Check to make sure everyone in your group understands these guidelines. Then turn the page.

©1994 Whole Person Press 210 W Michigan Duluth MN 55802   (800) 247-6789

> *A observes; B and C dialogue; B shares first* **3**
> *5 minutes*
>
> In this first 5-minute segment, B and C will practice good listening skills as they take turns responding to three topics. A acts as observer.
>
> **TOPIC 1: One stress I've experienced today is . . .**
>
> > **B** shares first.
> >
> > **C** responds empathically.
> >
> > > Pause to digest the answer, reflect on it, and paraphrase what your partner has said.
> > >
> > > Ask if your perception is accurate. If not, try again.
> > >
> > > When B feels that you have understood her response, switch roles and repeat the process, with C sharing and B listening.
> >
> > **A** should observe without commenting.
>
> Use the same process with the next two topics:
>
> **I coped with it (the stress you just shared) by . . .**
> **When I'm under stress, my body lets me know by . . .**
>
> > *Wait for instructions before turning the page.*
> > *Feel free to review the listening guidelines on page 2 at any time.*

> *B observes; A and C dialogue; C shares first* **4**
> *5 minutes*
>
> In this segment, you will practice listening as you discuss your own experience with listening.
>
> > **Tell your partner about an instance when someone listened to you empathically and whole-heartedly. What do you remember about how it felt?**
> >
> > > **C** answers first while **A** listens empathically. When C feels fully understood, switch roles: A answers the question and C listens.
> > >
> > > **B** observes without comment, making mental notes on the listening process.
>
> Use the same format in responding to the next question.
>
> > **When do you especially want to be listened to and heard?**
>
> > *The trainer will tell you when to go on.*
> > *If you have extra time, B and C can answer the last question again.*

C observes; A and B dialogue; A shares first   **5**
10 minutes

Now **C** gets to observe the listening process while **A** and **B** dialogue on the following three topics.

Don't forget to practice the good listening guidelines:
  show interest, reach out to understand, focus on your partner, and respond by periodically checking your perceptions.

Situations where I find it hard to listen . . .

People I have trouble listening to . . .

Describe a recent situation when you had difficulty listening or didn't want to listen (eg, argument, criticism, assignment, challenge, request, instructions, angry outburst, whining, etc).

  What did you **WANT** to hear?
  What did you hear **AT THE TIME?**
  In retrospect, what did **THE OTHER PERSON** really want to communicate?

Wait for the signal to move ahead.

A observes; B and C dialogue; C shares first   **6**
5 minutes each; 10 minutes total

Practice supportive listening by paraphrasing and responding with understanding. Take your time. **C** shares first while **B** listens empathically. Switch roles after about 5 minutes.

SHARER: **Describe a situation at home or work that upsets you.**

LISTENER: Listen and respond empathically.

  Show interest. Try to get inside your partner's shoes and understand the situation from his perspective.

  Don't give advice. Don't make judgments—not even positive ones. Don't ask questions that would throw your partner off. Don't problem-solve or reassure.

  DO reach out for the feelings and the meanings behind the words. DO summarize what you've heard and check out your perceptions. If they are inaccurate, try again until you've heard your partner fully.

Wait for the signal to move ahead.

C observes; A and B dialogue; B shares first
5 minutes

7

Paraphrase techniques also work well in conflict situations!
With your partner, **A** and **B**:

**Find a topic about which you DISAGREE
(eg, age for toilet training, men with pierced ears, nuclear
disarmament, politics, best brand of detergent, who will win the
Super Bowl, etc).**

Dialogue about this topic for 5 minutes, using the paraphrase rule:

**Each of you must restate your partner's position to her
satisfaction before you can air your own views.**

Use this rule throughout the discussion.

If your viewpoint has not been heard, ask your partner to listen again
until you really feel your partner understands your position.

When listening, remember to suspend your judgment and biases. Stay
open to hearing the other person's perspective.

Wait for the signal to go on.

8

STOP   Take a deep breath.

LOOK   Around the room and find another trio you'd like to talk with.
Join with them to make a sextet.

LISTEN   To each other as you take 5 minutes to share insights and
reactions to this experience.

As observers, what did you notice about listening?

When sharing, how did it feel to be heard? How accurately did your
partner listen and understand?

How difficult was it to **listen**? When?

Was there any difference in empathy with a supportive versus a conflict
situaiton?

Were there any surprises?

This was a stressful situation. How did listening work as a coper for you?

Wait for further instructions.

©1994 Whole Person Press 210 W Michigan Duluth MN 55802   (800) 247-6789

93 CENTERING MEDITATION

Participants experience the quieting process of meditation and the focusing power of visualization in this guided fantasy.

GOALS

To learn the principles of meditation and imagery as skills for relaxation.

To experience quiet, calm, peace and a sense of inner vision.

GROUP SIZE

Unlimited.

TIME FRAME

25–40 minutes

MATERIALS

Blank paper for all; soothing soft music.

PROCESS

1) The trainer introduces the exercise by describing the importance of relaxation as an antidote to stress—both as a remedy and as a preventive measure.

2) The trainer notes that this skill-building experience uses elements of two powerful techniques for inducing a relaxed state. He then goes on to describe the process and power of *meditation* and *guided imagery:*

   - *Meditation* may be the most wholistic of all stress management skills since it involves sensory awareness, physical relaxation, surrender of thought processes and focusing on the "life force" through breathing and contemplation.

   - The key elements needed for effective meditation include:
     - A *quiet environment* that's free from distraction;
     - A *comfortable position* that can be maintained easily for 20 minutes;
     - A *phrase, sound* or *object to focus on* so that distracting thoughts will pass; and
     - An open and *passive attitude*, accepting whatever the experience brings.

- Scientists have discovered that the **hypothalamus** (the area of the brain that gathers information input from the senses) responds to **symbolic** stimuli almost as well as to the real thing. Just as a terrifying movie can provoke our stress reactions, visualizing a peaceful scene will calm our bodies down!

- If we practice, we can learn to trigger the relaxation response almost instantly just by using our imaginations.

3) The trainer invites participants to join in the centering meditation and describes the activity:

➤ This relaxation routine combines breathing, **visual imagery** and some aspects of **meditation** in a process of physical and mental centering.

➤ The first part consists of a quieting process to get our energy centered. We will then take an imaginary walk in the forest.

➤ The last step involves some writing. Everyone will need to have paper and pencil handy so as not to disrupt the mood.

4) The trainer instructs participants to relax in their chairs and close their eyes. He turns on the soft music he has selected and slowly reads the **Centering Meditation** script.

☞ *Be sure to read the script very slowly. To pace yourself, take a deep breath at every "..." and pause between sections. Leave the music playing softly in the background, while participants write down their conversations.*

5) After he has completed reading the script, the trainer allows several minutes (3–10) for people to write their dialogues. He then asks participants to complete the portion they are working on and return their attention to the group.

6) Finally, the trainer invites any who are willing to read their dialogues aloud to the entire group.

☞ *Reading these dialogues aloud can be an extremely powerful process. Be patient and wait for volunteers. Do not let people talk about or explain their dialogues. Ask them to read what they have written without additional comment. Do not comment or permit discussion. Simply listen to the dialogue, thank the sharer and move to the next. When all who wish to read their dialogues have done so, this exercise is concluded.*

©1994 Whole Person Press 210 W Michigan Duluth MN 55802   (800) 247-6789

CENTERING MEDITATION Script

We are sitting in quiet . . . and calm . . .
Letting the core become clear . . .
Letting the thoughts slow their pace . . .
Letting the breath become regular and slow . . .
Letting the self become still . . .

We are sitting in quiet . . . and calm . . .
Letting the breath become steady and deep . . .
Letting energies that were once chasing madly
focus inward and rest . . .
within the stillness of our center . . .
Letting energies come to rest
upon the steady rhythm of our breathing . . .

Breathing at the center, our breath becomes deeper . . .
Breathing at the quiet and calm of our core
our breath becomes pure and clear . . .

Our breathing is free . . . and regular . . .
Our breathing finds it easy to come . . . and go . . .
on its own . . . without our effort . . .

Our thoughts become quiet . . .
Wandering thoughts come to rest . . .
Our feelings become one . . . one flow of experience . . .
All rests on the regular rhythm of our steady breathing . . .
that moves into our soul . . .
Bringing peace . . . and quiet . . .
Bringing healing to our core . . .

We are centered . . . we are quiet . . .
All parts connected . . .
Connected together . . . by the rhythm of our steady breathing . . .

We are clear . . . and we know clearly . . . and deeply . . .
We know peace . . .
As breathing moves . . . in . . . and out . . .
at the center of our being . . .
The core . . . waits calmly . . .
for the quiet . . . of the breathing . . .
to bring it healing life . . .

I am aware of seeing beyond my eyes . . .
of hearing with more than my ears . . .
of knowing outside of my mind . . .
I see and know truth at the core of my being . . .
And I wait . . . and watch . . . in quiet . . . and calm . . .
Aware only of my steady, regular breathing . . .

©1994 Whole Person Press 210 W Michigan Duluth MN 55802   (800) 247-6789

As I wait . . . I find myself in a forest . . .
A forest of trees spread far apart with large trunks . . .
The trees are so tall they soar above me . . .
The huge canopy of branches overlapping as a ceiling to cover me
and block out the bright sunlight . . .

The sun shining so brightly above . . .
cannot get through to the forest floor where I stand . . .
Where I walk it is dark . . .
Where I walk on the floor of the forest . . . it is quiet . . .

The quiet surrounds me . . . as I listen to the stillness . . .
The silence follows me . . . as I move slowly through the forest . . .

I listen to the presence around me . . .
I feel the power of the quiet that surrounds me . . .
And I know I am no longer alone . . .

As I watch . . . I notice a small bush . . .
It is unlike anything else in the forest . . .
It is glowing . . . gently . . .
Its glowing lights up the darkness of the forest . . .
As it hovers . . . barely touching the ground . . .

It glows before me . . .
Its flowers twinkle with a special light
and its glowing is strong . . . and even . . .
Showing no signs of diminishing . . .
Showing no source of power . . .
The bush glows . . .
with a soft brightness . . . that comes from within . . .

I am standing deep in the forest . . .
It is dark at the floor of the forest . . .
But I am touched . . . and surrounded by a soft light
that comes from the bush . . .
It reaches me . . . touches me . . . gently . . .

I feel the soft quality of being that comes from its light . . .
I am touched by a gentle power that does not diminish . . .
The glowing bush is part of me . . .
It glows within me . . .
It enters my heart . . . and burns steadily . . .

The glowing bush in the woods bathes me with its soft light . . .
The bush will stay with me . . .

The glowing bush enlightens my core
at the very center of my being . . .
where my breathing maintains its regular steady rhythm . . .
At this center of my being the bush lights my heart . . .
and shows me truth . . .

As I stand before the bush my center is quiet . . .
*   and calm . . . My center is light . . .*
As I stand before it . . .
*   I become aware I am no longer alone . . .*
*   A wise and kind person is with me . . . one whom I trust . . .*
*   A wise person . . . very gentle and caring . . .*
*   In the quiet . . . the wise one speaks to me . . .*
*   Speaks about the bush . . . about life . . . about me . . .*
*   And I listen . . . And I respond . . .*
And the wise one speaks . . .
*   And I listen . . . and respond . . .*
*   Speaking . . . and listening . . .*
*   Listening . . . and speaking . . .*
As our dialogue continues . . .
*   I experience the growing of wisdom in me . . .*
*   Wisdom . . . from my friend . . . from the bush . . .*
*   from within me . . .*
*   A clarity and knowledge of truth grows in me . . .*
Listening . . . and speaking . . . speaking and listening . . .
*   I am being touched . . .*

☞ *Pause*

As you are ready . . .
*   slowly come back into the room,*
*   just enough to make some notes of the dialogue . . .*
*   between you and your wise friend . . .*
Write it like a play with your friend speaking first . . .
*   and then write your response . . .*

☞ *Pause 20-30 seconds*

As you are ready . . .
*   slowly come back into the room*
*   just enough to make some notes of the dialogue*
*   between you and your wise friend . . .*
*   Write it like a play with your friend speaking first*
*   and then write your response . . .*

☞ *Pause 3-10 minutes while people write*

Take just a minute now
*   to finish up whatever you're working on . . .*
*   Then return your attention to this room . . .*

Planning
& Closure

94 CLOSING FORMATION

In this round-robin ending participants pair up with many different partners to briefly share reactions, insights and coping plans.

GOALS

To review highlights of the learning experience.

To touch base with many other participants before ending the session/ course.

To solidify specific plans for better stress management.

GROUP SIZE

Works best with 16 or more people, but can be adapted for smaller groups.

TIME FRAME

10–30 minutes.

PROCESS

1) The trainer asks participants to stand up and quickly find a partner— perhaps the person in an adjacent seat. As soon as everyone is paired, she gives instructions.

   ➤ Spend 1 minute brainstorming together, identifying the most important points covered during the course/session.

2) Pairs are instructed to find another pair and join together as a foursome. As soon as the groups have gathered, the trainer announces the topic.

   ➤ You will have 2 minutes to talk about the most exciting ideas/ concepts/attitudes/skills you have learned. Each person will get a chance to share your favorite.

3) The trainer calls time and explains the next formation (see diagram).

   ➤ Choose another quartet and join to form a double circle, one group back to back in the middle (*A's*) and the other group on the outside, facing the center (*B's*).

   ➤ People in the outside group (*B's*) should position yourselves so that everyone is facing a partner in the inside group.

☞ *If the group does not divide evenly into eights, see suggestions under* **Variation**.

4) The trainer chooses a sentence stub from the **Closing Formation Prompts**, reads it to the group and gives instructions to participants.

➤ With your partners, share the first response that comes to mind.

5) After 1 minute, the trainer calls time and directs all the people in outside groups (**B's**) to shift *one person to the right*, finding a new partner. She chooses another sentence stub and asks participants to share their "off the top of the head" responses.

This process is repeated two more times, using different prompts. By now all the *A's* in one formation have shared with all the *B's.*

6) The trainer asks all the *A's* in the room to stay put where they are, while each outside group of *B's* moves on to a new group of *A's*, making a new formation.

☞ *This can be a chaotic process with a large group. Help them out by deciding which group of B's should go where (eg, move to the next group—to your left, toward the windows, or counter clockwise, etc), and directing them verbally and non-verbally.*

Step 4 is repeated in the new formation, rotating partners and using a new sentence stub for each new partner.

7) The trainer invites participants to return to their seats and solicits observations and insights from the group before making her own closing remarks.

8) In conclusion the trainer may ask people to write a summary of the ideas and personal resolutions that they want to remember and take home from this experience.

VARIATION

■ If the group does not divide evenly into 8's, the process can be adapted to groups of 3 and 6. Or after *Step 1* pairs could line up (as for a Virginia reel): one line stays stationery while the other moves one person to the right after each prompt/response sequence. Continue until the group seems to be tiring.

CLOSING FORMATION

■ *One thing I learned about myself in this course is . . .*

■ *I am still confused about . . .*

■ *The part of this experience I liked best is . . .*

■ *One thing I particularly liked about the trainer/leader is . . .*

■ *One thing I will tell other people about this experience is . . .*

■ *Something I've noticed about your coping style is . . .*

■ *One thing I appreciate about myself as a participant is . . .*

■ *One personal resolution I've made is . . .*

■ *The most surprising thing I've discovered here is . . .*

■ *The most disturbing insight I've had is . . .*

■ *One way I've learned I'm like most other people here is . . .*

■ *One way I've learned I'm unique from others here is . . .*

■ *One situation where I know I need to use what I've learned . . .*

■ *One personal discovery I've made is . . .*

■ *The best way to manage stress is . . .*

■ *The person in my environment who will benefit most from what I've learned is . . .*

95 EXIT INTERVIEW

In dyads participants review course content and publicly affirm their plans for improved stress management.

GOALS

To reinforce concepts and techniques presented during the learning experience.

To provide closure.

To articulate plans for integrating and implementing stress management principles in daily life.

GROUP SIZE

Unlimited as long as there is space for pairs to find privacy.

TIME FRAME

20–30 minutes; longer with a large group.

MATERIALS NEEDED

Ted Koppel and **Barbara Walters Interview Outlines** for each dyad.

PROCESS

1) The trainer instructs participants to find a partner with whom to share this closing experience.

   ☞ *If participants have stayed in the same small group during the learning experience, encourage them to choose someone outside that group as a partner. This facilitates transition and reentry to the "real world."*

2) After everyone is settled, the trainer explains the exit interview process.

   ➤ Partners will be interviewing each other about what you have learned during the course and how you hope to apply it in your real life situations.

   ➤ Decide who will be *Ted Koppel* and who will be *Barbara Walters.*

3) The trainer distributes **Ted Koppel** and **Barbara Walters Interview Outlines** to the appropriate person in each dyad and gives specific instructions.

➤ Alternate asking questions.

> ***Barbara Walters*** should ask the first question from your outline and make brief notes of your partner's response.

> Then ***Ted Koppel*** should ask the first question from your outline and notes your partner's response.

> ***Barbara*** goes next with your second question, and then ***Ted*** asks your second.

➤ Continue this process until all questions have been posed and answered.

➤ The whole sequence should take about 15 minutes.

☞ *Remind people that to understand what their partner is saying is much more important than getting all the words down. A quick review of good listening skills (attending behavior, paraphrasing, open-ended questioning, etc) might be helpful.*

4) After about 10 minutes the trainer announces that there are 5 minutes left.

➤ Some of you may need to speed up the process to get to the final questions.

➤ If you finish early, go back and explore some questions in more depth.

5) The trainer calls time and asks participants to spend 3 minutes writing a few sentences briefly summarizing the highlights shared by the person they interviewed.

6) In closing, participants read these summaries out loud to the whole group. The trainer acknowledges each contribution and closes with an affirmation of the exciting growth and learning they have shared together.

☞ *Encourage partners to exchange interview papers to take home as souvenirs and reminders about their insights and resolutions for change.*

BARBARA WALTERS
Interview Outline

A. Let's talk for a moment about the most interesting, surprising aspects of your learning experience. What really caught your attention?

B. Speaking personally, based on your history with the issue of stress, which specific coping methods do you think would be most helpful for you to learn? . . . And how do you think this would help you avoid some of the troublesome spots you've gotten yourself into in the past?

C. I know that you have a reputation for keeping your plans secret, but won't you please give us a glimpse of the personal management plan for stress you hammered out during this session?

D. As you well know, sabotage of our own good intentions is the most prevalent force preventing positive change in people. How are you most likely to sabotage your new plans for managing stress? . . . And what steps have you taken to prevent yourself from sabotaging your own good intentions?

SUMMARY

TED KOPPEL
Interview Outline

A. Would you focus for a moment on some of the most meaningful and helpful learnings you gained from this course? What will you take home? What strikes you as most significant?

B. Would you explain clearly for our viewers at home the aspect of stress management you believe is most difficult to understand and to put into practice?

C. Some would say that while stress courses provide an elixir to help people feel good, that in the end these courses don't ever do much good—because, these same critics point out, people never really change their bad habits. In the light of your recent training what would you say to these allegations? . . . And specifically, what changes, if any, are you prepared to make on the basis of your learning here?

D. Now that you have this course under your belt, what do you need to do next? How are you planning to accomplish this?

SUMMARY

©1994 Whole Person Press 210 W Michigan Duluth MN 55802   (800) 247-6789

96 RECIPE FOR SUCCESS

Participants reflect on the ingredients for successful stress management as they cook up innovative personal recipes for handling stress.

GOALS

To review qualities that are particularly effective in coping with stress.

To promote creativity, humor and self-expression.

GROUP SIZE

Unlimited.

TIME FRAME

25–30 minutes

MATERIALS

Recipe for Success with Stress forms for all participants.

PROCESS

☞ *Before using this exercise with a group, create two or three sample recipes of your own that will serve as examples (eg, "Take one harried Type A person, add two tons of patience and a dollop of humor, mix vigorously and set in the sun to rest for 3 days. Then massage vigorously, stir in a gallon of values clarification, a pound of faith and a pinch of play. Sprinkle with forgiveness and let it breathe!")*

1) The trainer announces that this closing exercise will give everyone a chance to play the role of expert by creating a secret recipe for success with stress. He distributes **Recipe for Success with Stress** forms to all and describes the process.

➤ You can make up whatever ingredients, proportions and directions you believe would make a good stress manager.

➤ Write your description in the format of a cookbook recipe or a recipe card.

☞ *To help the group get going, you may want to generate lists of typical as well as serious measurements (eg, cups, oodles, a scant teaspoon) and directions (eg, combine, toss together, pour in, or cool off). Encourage people to think seriously about what they have learned about coping with stress and then to be as imaginative, creative, and zany as they can in writing their recipe for success.*

2) One by one, participants read their recipes to the group.

3) The trainer summarizes the characteristics included in the recipes and uses them as a springboard to review positive strategies for managing stress.

VARIATIONS

■ Recipes could be collected, duplicated and compiled in a cookbook for distribution to all participants. This serves as a good follow-up reminder of the learning experience.

■ If the group is larger than 20 people and time is limited, participants could form smaller groups (10–16 people) for sharing recipes.

■ Recipes could be written for specific situations such as "success with managing change" or "handling conflict" or "being assertive" or "dealing with difficult people."

TRAINER'S NOTES

Submitted by Mark Warner.

Stress

Recipe for _Success with Stress_   **From the Kitchen of** _____

_____

_____

_____

_____

_____

_____

_____

_____

_____

_____

_____

97 STRESS REDUCTION PROGRAM

This step-by-step planning process helps participants formulate a specific plan for managing a stress-related problem.

GOALS

To practice a process for developing a stress management program tailored to deal with specific stressors.

To elicit personal commitment to change.

TIME FRAME

20–30 minutes

MATERIALS

My Stress Reduction Program worksheets for all.

PROCESS

1) Participants are invited to reflect privately on the sources of stress in their lives and to make a list of specific stressors and/or stressful patterns they would like to change.

    ☞ *To prime the pump give several examples of a wide range of stressors, including some that participants have mentioned earlier in the learning experience (eg, overeating, financial instability, hassles with the baby-sitter, death in the family, illness, poor self-image, noisy office, etc).*

2) The trainer distributes **My Stress Reduction Program** worksheets and asks everyone to choose one stress-maker to focus on for the remainder of the exercise.

    In answering the first question on the worksheet, participants are instructed to describe the stressor briefly. The trainer then guides the group through the rest of the planning process, giving examples as needed and adjusting the pace to the rhythm of the group.

3) The trainer asks participants to share examples of their personal stress reduction programs and closes by reminding everyone that this same process can be used to develop a strategy for any stressor.

Submitted by Jim Cathcart.

MY STRESS REDUCTION PROGRAM

1) This is the problem:

Example: not getting enough exercise

2) This is what I can do about it:

Example: change my schedule to exercise 3 hours per week

3) This is what I'm doing now that needs to be changed:

Example: when I come home, I get a drink and sit down

4) This is what I could do instead:

Example: play racquetball at noon; take bus to work; join health club and work out at night

5) This is what I will do:

Example: take a brisk walk instead of a cocktail

6) This is my goal:

Example: four weeks from today I'll be able to walk easily for 30 minutes after work

7) This is how I'll reward myself when I reach my goal:

Example: buy new stereo speakers

8) This is how I'll work my plan: (how often? where? when?)

Example: Every day after work I'll walk to the park 3 miles from home. I won't have a drink after work, starting today.

9) This is the result(s) that I expect:

Example: reduced alcohol consumption, increased aerobic capacity

10) This is how I'll evaluate my progress:

Example: pulse checks, logging mileage, daily weigh-in, recording alcohol intake

©1994 Whole Person Press 210 W Michigan Duluth MN 55802   (800) 247-6789

98 CHANGE PENTAGON

Participants explore each aspect of life (mental, physical, spiritual, inter-personal and lifestyle) seeking positive alternatives for managing stress. They then draw up a "whole person" plan for dealing with specific problem situations.

GOALS

To isolate stressful situations that require attention.

To expand awareness of coping options in each dimension of life that might reduce stress.

To make a plan for coping in a new way with a stressful situation.

GROUP SIZE

Unlimited; works well with individuals, too.

TIME FRAME

15–30 minutes

MATERIALS

Several **Change Pentagon** worksheet for each participant.

PROCESSWORKSHEET

1) The trainer distributes one (or more) **Change Pentagon** worksheet to each participant, and invites people to consider what changes they might like to make in their management of stress.

   ➤ Mentally review the issues that have come up for you during the learning experience.

   ➤ Identify several stress-provoking situations or patterns that you would like to alter. Choose one to focus on and write it in the center circle of your worksheet.

2) The trainer talks participants through the process of investigating each of the five life areas for changes they could make that might help them manage this particular stress-provoking pattern or situation more effectively.

➤ *Physical changes.* Do you want to make any alterations in exercise? Diet? Environment? Sleep? Routine? Pace? Relaxation? Record any desired changes in the *physical changes* section of the worksheet.

➤ *Thinking/feeling changes.* What different perceptions or ideas might be helpful? What about changes in attitudes? Opinions? Feelings? In the *thinking/feeling* section of your worksheet jot down ways you might want to change your mental response to this situation.

➤ *Changes in relationships.* What about your friends? Family? Communication patterns? Conflict resolution? Use the *relationship* section to write down your ideas about interpersonal changes you might want to make.

➤ *Spiritual changes.* What alterations in faith might be helpful? Values? Meditation/prayer life? Note any *spiritual* changes that might impact this stress.

➤ *Lifestyle changes.* What changes in focus and commitments are needed? Daily, weekly, yearly patterns? Lifework satisfaction? Long-term and short-term goals? Community service? Record your answers in the *lifestyle* triangle.

☞ *If time allows, repeat the process with one or more additional stress-provoking situations, using a new worksheet for each.*

3) The trainer invites participants to join two other people and brainstorm together about additional changes that they might make in the different areas of life to manage their stress-provokers better.

4) Participants are invited to make a plan for implementing change.

➤ Review all the suggestions for positive change you have listed for each different stress-provoking situation.

➤ At the bottom of each worksheet select the changes you want to make and write a personal plan of action to deal with that particular stress.

5) The trainer invites those participants who wish to read their plans out loud to the group.

CHANGE PENTAGON

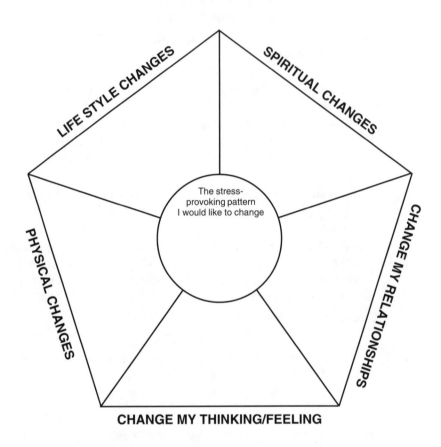

MY PLAN OF ACTION:

(800) 247-6789

Group
Energizers

99 KICKING YOUR STRESS CAN-CAN

In this invigorating dance routine participants kick up their heels as they symbolically kick sources of stress out of their lives.

GOALS

To demonstrate exercise as a pleasurable and effective stress-reducer.

To target specific stressors for change.

TIME FRAME

5 minutes or longer

MATERIALS

Can-Can (Offenbach's "Orpheus in the Underworld," Andre Previn's "Gaite Parisienne") or other lively dance music.

PROCESS

1) The trainer invites participants to think of several stressful situations, people, attitudes, events, etc that they would like to "kick out" of their life right now. (Or consult a list of stressors generated earlier in the learning experience.)

2) The trainer asks everyone to get up and move around in the room so that all have plenty of space to dance and kick.

   ☞ *If the room is fairly crowded, have people form lines, shoulder to shoulder, to maximize space.*

3) The trainer demonstrates the Kicking Your Stress Can-Can step.

   ➤ Hop on left foot, bringing right knee up to chest;

   ➤ Hop on left foot, tapping right on the floor;

   ➤ Hop on left foot, kicking right foot out front;

   ➤ Hop on left foot, tapping right on the floor;

   ☞ *Repeat this sequence 4 times. Then change to hopping on **right** foot, kicking **left**.*

   ➤ Repeat 4 times then alternate to other foot.

4) The trainer starts the music and invites participants to dance, visualizing that with every kick they are booting a troublesome stressor out of their life.

---

100 CHINESE SWING

In this invigorating exercise break participants learn an ancient oriental technique for releasing stress.

GOALS

To stimulate energy flow in the body and to promote deep breathing.

To discharge muscular tension.

GROUP SIZE

Unlimited as long as there is space for all to swing their arms without obstruction.

TIME FRAME

10 minutes

PROCESS

1) The trainer introduces The Swing, summarizing the following points:

   ● This is an ancient Chinese exercise which seems to have a power similar to acupressure for generating energy or *"chi,"* particularly in the lower body organs.

   ● The Swing is especially good for people who work in offices since when we are sitting, all the organs below the lungs are pressed together and the energy cannot circulate well in the lower trunk and legs.

   ● Proponents of The Swing claim that this exercise can lead to improvement in general muscle tone and digestive functioning, increased circulatory efficiency, and relief of mental and physical tensions.

     ☞ *You might joke, "Well, even if it doesn't give us all of those benefits, at least this exercise will get us up and moving, and give us an enjoyable break. Who knows—some of you may even be instantly healed by this powerful tool!"*

2) Participants are invited to stand and spread out around the room so that everyone is free to swing their arms forward and backward without bumping anything. The trainer demonstrates as he describes the stance and the Swing technique:

> Stand with your feet apart, at shoulder width. Let your arms hang loosely at your sides, palms facing backward.

> Hold the belly in and the upper body erect; relax your neck by lowering it forward.

> Grasp the floor with toes and heels and tighten the muscles of your legs and thighs so that you feel most of your weight centered in the lower part of your body.

> Focus your eyes on a selected point at least ten feet away, and relax your mind.

> To start, force your arms backward as far as possible. Then let them swing freely forward by the force of gravity until they reach a natural position at about a 60-degree angle in front of your body.

3) As soon as everyone catches on, the trainer asks people to start counting their swings and keep on until they reach 100–150 repetitions, paying particular attention to any bodily sensations that they experience.

4) When almost all are finished, the trainer solicits reactions from the group.

✔ What sensations did you experience?

✔ Do you feel energized or fatigued?

✔ What happened to your tension level?

5) In closing, the trainer describes the recommended daily dosage of Chinese Swing.

● Begin with 150 repetitions of the exercise. After the second week, add 20 each day until you can do 1,000 repetitions, which takes about 30 minutes.

● After swinging 200–300 times you may experience gas, hiccups, sweat, flush and even feel sore in the legs. These are signs that the digestion is starting to function better and the energy is circulating throughout the body organs.

● Don't tire yourself by overdoing it! For maximum benefit, do the Swing outside in the fresh air.

Submitted by Mary O'Brien Sippel.

101 CLOUDS TO SUNSHINE

This adaptation of a traditional T'ai Chi exercise allows participants to breathe and stretch easily while imagining four different scenes from nature.

GOALS

To focus attention and let go of mental distractions.

To stretch and release tension from the muscles in the arms and back.

GROUP SIZE

Unlimited, as long as there is space to stretch comfortably.

TIME FRAME

3–5 minutes; may be repeated several times.

PROCESS

☞ *Be sure to practice this sequence ahead of time so you can describe and demonstrate it easily.*

1) The trainer invites participants to stand and join in a revitalizing stretch based upon traditional T'ai Chi movements.

2) The trainer demonstrates as she reads the instructions for the **Clouds—Rain—Rainbow—Sunshine** exercise sequence.

☞ *You may want to add to the scene by suggesting that participants imagine that there is a pool or pond of water evaporating on a warm day. The energy flows up as the moisture rises and the participants lift their arms toward the sky.*

3) Participants repeat the sequence one or more times.

Submitted by Marti Belknap.

CLOUDS—RAIN—RAINBOW—SUNSHINE

CLOUDS

Stand with your knees relaxed and your hands cupped in front of your pelvis.

Inhale and draw energy up from the earth through your body.

Invert your hands and **push the clouds** toward the sky.

RAIN

Exhale and lower your arms in an arc down to your sides.

Allow the **rain to fall** gently upon the earth.

RAINBOW

Clasp your hands together behind your back and lift your arms as you **inhale.**

Exhale and bend forward with your arms extended behind you.

Form a rainbow with your body over the land. Inhale and lift. Relax arms to sides and **exhale**.

SUNSHINE

Turn your palms upward and lift your arms in an arc overhead as you **inhale**.

Exhale and embrace the sunshine with your arms making a circle in front of your chest.

Inhale and **draw the sunshine** into your heart. **Exhale** and feel the sun bathe your body.

102 CREATE-A-SINGALONG

Participants compose stress and coping lyrics for familiar melodies and then perform their "work" for the group.

GOALS

To reinforce concepts taught in the session or course.

To promote group creativity and spontaneity.

GROUP SIZE

Unlimited.

TIME FRAME

10–15 minutes; longer with larger groups.

MATERIALS

Newsprint or overhead transparencies.

PROCESS

1) The trainer announces that during the next 10 minutes everyone will have an opportunity to demonstrate their creative abilities by helping to compose a song that incorporates something they have learned about stress or coping during this course (session/workshop).

2) The trainer divides participants into small groups of 3–6 persons and assigns each group a different tune to use as the melody (eg, *Three Blind Mice; Row Your Boat; Silent Night; America; Frere Jacques; Twinkle, Twinkle Little Star;* school fight songs, etc).

   ☞ *You may want to give an example like the following to prime the pump and get the humor flowing —*

   (Tune: Three Blind Mice)

   Much less stress! Much less stress!
   We've all learned how to cope with it,
   Not eat or drink or smoke with it!
   Just breathe and stretch and joke with it!
   Much less stress! Much less stress!

3) The trainer provides each group with newsprint or overhead transparencies and markers to use in recording their final lyrics for all to see.

4) After about 10 minutes the trainer notifies groups that there are only a few minutes left and encourages them to get their songs recorded.

☞ *You may need to remind people that the songs don't have to be perfect—just fun!*

5) As soon as the groups are ready the trainer asks each in turn to come up front and teach their song to the others, demonstrating it first and then inviting all participants to join in the singing.

6) After all have "performed," the may want to choose one of the creations as their special theme song to be repeated periodically throughout the rest of the learning experience.

TRAINER'S NOTES

103 GROANS AND MOANS

In this noisy energizer participants experiment with groaning, an old-fashioned remedy for stress.

GOALS

To demonstrate the effectiveness of groaning as a tension-relieving technique.

To relax and let go.

GROUP SIZE

Unlimited; it may be difficult to persuade a very small group or an especially formal one to try this technique.

TIME FRAME

15 minutes

MATERIALS

Tape recorder, recording of soulful instrumental jazz such as Coltrane, Brubek, Miles Davis, etc.

SETTING

Works especially well when the room is carpeted and participants can spread out on the floor, but the exercise can also be done seated in chairs.

PROCESS

1) The trainer invites participants to experiment with a natural, easy, healthy, old-fashioned technique for dealing with unavoidable pain, emotional pressures and stress—groaning. As participants groan in disbelief at her announcement, she continues by outlining several benefits of the therapeutic groan.

   ● Groaning helps you relax physically by stimulating deep, regulated breathing, maximizing oxygen intake and exercising the diaphragm.

   ● As you relax, the vibrations of the groan in your throat, chest and sinuses provide a tension-shedding internal massage.

   ● The process of groaning creates a focus for concentration that can still the restless mind.

2) The trainer invites participants to stretch out comfortably on the floor or in their chairs. Once everyone is settled, she demonstrates several deep, full-bodied groans and gives instructions for effective groaning.

> It's perfectly normal to feel a little silly and embarrassed, at least at first—and it's OK to giggle!

> Close your eyes and start groaning.

>> To avoid straining your voice, the flow of air from the windpipe should not be restricted.

>> Experiment, moving your head until you find the position where your groan is most open-flowing and effortless, even when the sound is quite loud.

☞ *You may want to play some "soul music" to ease embarassment and help cover the uproar.*

3) The trainer announces that the group will practice groaning for 5 or 10 minutes—and then encourages, prods, cajoles, challenges, and cheers participants as necessary to get them going and to help them through the first moments of giggling and confusion.

☞ *Be sure to keep groaning with the group so they don't run out of steam. With a potentially resistant group it helps to have a conspirator planted in the audience to help.*

4) After 7–10 minutes of deep groaning (the more, the better) the trainer invites people to slowly and gently return their awareness to the room and describe their experiences. As people share, the trainer uses the data generated to highlight the potential benefits and applications of groaning:

● A groan can be used as a pressure valve to deal with a stress overload by releasing a strong overflow of pressure or pain while it's still building up.

● Any time you need temporary relief of tension, exhaustion or other emotional pain, you can simply groan!

● The incongruity of humor and laughter that sometimes arises in the midst of groaning can provide enjoyable—and perhaps healing—relief!

Submitted by Louis M Savary.

104 TUG OF WAR

In this game of strategy, participants pair up to explore alternative approaches to conflict.

GOALS

To assist individuals in obtaining a glimpse of their personal style at approaching conflict.

GROUP SIZE

Minimum of 8–10 people.

TIME FRAME

5–10 minutes

PROCESS

1) The trainer defines conflict and announces that during the next 5 minutes participants will join in an experiment to discover/rediscover how they typically approach conflict situations. She then asks everyone to stand up and find a partner.

2) Once everyone has a partner, the trainer gives each pair a piece of paper and describes the **Tug of War.**

  ➤ Decide who should hold the paper.

   ☞ *"Playfair" techniques could be substituted here. Instead of asking partners to decide who should hold the paper, ask them to decide who is the zucchini and who is the artichoke (or who is the penguin and who is the flamingo, etc). You can then announce that the zucchinis (or penguins) will hold the paper first.*

  ➤ The person holding the paper should hold on to it and not let go under any circumstances.

  ➤ The person NOT holding the paper should attempt to get the paper from your partner, using any strategy you can imagine.

  ➤ You will have exactly one minute to accomplish this task.

☞ *During the exercise observe closely and note interactions that illustrate different styles of resolving conflict situations (eg, some people will grab, others will wheedle or sweet talk and some may even offer cash).*

3) After one minute the trainer calls time and asks participants to switch roles and repeat the exercise.

4) At the end of one minute, time is called and the trainer invites participants to describe what they noticed about their style of approaching a conflict situation.

TRAINER'S NOTES

Submitted by Jan Berry-Schroeder.

105 WARM HANDS

In this brief introduction to the potential of autogenics, participants imagine their way to warm hands and a profound sense of relaxation.

GOALS

To demonstrate the power of autogenic-like techniques for relaxation.

GROUP SIZE

Unlimited; works well with individuals, too.

TIME FRAME

5–10 minutes

PROCESS

1) The trainer invites participants to experiment with an effective relaxation technique that is based on visualization and autogenics—a process of self-regulation that uses mental imagery and the power of suggestion to counteract the physical side effects of stress.

   ☞ *You might warn participants that if anyone feels anxious or uncomfortable during the experience, they should stop the imagery process at once and take a break.*

2) The trainer gives directions for "warming up" to relaxation.

   ➤ Assume a tension-free position. Sit with your arms supported on your thighs, hands between your knees, shoulders slightly shrugged, body balanced over your pelvis and eyes closed.

   ➤ Adopt an attitude of passive concentration, focusing on the words and images as they are suggested. Mentally repeat the phrase silently several times in the silence between images.

3) The trainer slowly reads the **Warm Hands** instructions, pausing long enough at each image so that people can mentally review the phrase two or three times before moving on.

   ☞ *Keep your voice steady and the pace even as you read. Try not to emphasize any words. It should sound monotonous!*

Submitted by David Danskin.

WARM HANDS Script

Let's begin by taking a deep breath.
Inhale, filling your lungs with air all the way down to the belly.
Now exhale slowly with a soft "whooshing" sound.
Take another deep breath . . . and imagine as you breathe out that all the tension is leaving your body . . .

Imagine your hands as warm — relaxed and warm . . .
Say to yourself slowly four times . . .
MY HANDS ARE WARM . . . RELAXED AND WARM . . . .

    ☞ *Pause 15 seconds*

Now visualize your hands in a bucket of warm water . . .
or near a roaring fire . . .
Stay with that image as you slowly say to yourself . . .
MY HANDS ARE WARM . . . RELAXED AND WARM . . .

    ☞ *Pause*

Make your mental image as vivid as possible as you warm your hands in this comfortable cozy way . . . reminding yourself again . . .
MY HANDS ARE WARM . . . RELAXED AND WARM . . .

    ☞ *Pause*

As you continue to visualize your hands becoming warmer and more relaxed . . . perhaps you can even begin to allow the blood to flow down your arms . . . and into your hands . . . leaving them feeling warmer and warmer . . . and more and more relaxed . . .
Let that feeling of warmth and relaxation spread down your arms and into your hands as you say to yourself . . .
MY HANDS ARE WARM . . . RELAXED AND WARM . . .

    ☞ *Pause*

Now allow that pleasant feeling of warmth to spread throughout your body as you tell yourself . . . I AM CALM AND RELAXED . . .

    ☞ *Pause*

Continue to enjoy this feeling of warmth and relaxation as you prepare to turn your attention from the inner you to the outer world . . .
Before you open your eyes . . . mentally prepare for your return by saying several times to yourself . . . WHEN I OPEN MY EYES I WILL FEEL RELAXED, FRESH AND ALERT . . .

    ☞ *Pause*

When you are ready . . . please open your eyes . . .

106 WHAT'S THE HURRY?

This touching parable points out how striving too hard to reach a goal may have stressful side effects.

GOALS

To help participants reflect on the potential risks of *Type A* behavior.

GROUP SIZE

Unlimited

TIME FRAME

5–10 minutes

PROCESS

☞ *This story will have a maximum impact if it is included to illustrate or top off a presentation on Type A behavior.*

1) The trainer reads the parable, **What's the Hurry?**

2) When the reading is finished and before the mood of the group is broken, the trainer may ask participants to write down a sentence or two describing the meaning and message of this parable in their current life situation.

3) After a few minutes for reflection, the trainer may ask for insights, observations and examples.

WHAT'S THE HURRY? Script

There once was a fellow who, with his father, farmed a little piece of land. Several times a year they'd load up the ox-cart with vegetables and drive to the nearest city.

Except for their names and the patch of ground, father and son had little in common. The old man believed in taking it easy . . . and the son was the go-getter type.

One morning, they loaded the cart, hitched up the ox and set out.

The young fellow figured that if they kept going all day and night, they'd get to the market by next morning. He walked alongside the ox and kept prodding it with a stick.

"Take it easy," said the old man. "You'll last longer."

"If we get to market ahead of the others," said his son, "we have a better chance of getting good prices."

The old man pulled his hat down over his eyes and went to sleep on the seat. Four miles and four hours down the road, they came to a little house.

"Here's your uncle's place," said the father, waking up. "Let's stop in and say hello."

"We've lost an hour already," complained the go-getter.

"Then a few minutes more won't matter," said his father. "My brother and I live so close, yet we see each other so seldom."

The young man fidgeted while the two old gentlemen gossiped away an hour.

On the move again, the father took his turn leading the ox. By and by, they came to a fork in the road. The old man directed the ox to the right.

"The left is the shorter way," said the boy.

"I know it," said the old man, "but this way is prettier."

"Have you no respect for time?" asked the impatient young man.

"I respect it very much," said the old fellow. "That's why I like to use it for looking at pretty things."

The right-hand path led through woodland and wild flowers. The young man was so busy watching the sun sink he didn't notice how lovely the sunset was.

Twilight found them in what looked like one big garden.

©1994 Whole Person Press 210 W Michigan Duluth MN 55802   (800) 247-6789

"Let's sleep here," said the old man.

"This is the last trip I take with you," snapped his son. "You're more interested in flowers than in making money."

"That's the nicest thing you've said in a long time," smiled the old fellow. A minute later he was asleep.

A little before sunrise, the young man shook his father awake. They hitched up and went on. A mile and an hour away they came upon a farmer trying to pull his cart out of a ditch.

"Let's give him a hand," said the father.

"And lose more time?" exploded the son.

"Relax," said the old man. "You might be in a ditch sometime yourself."

By the time the other cart was back on the road, it was almost eight o'clock. Suddenly a great flash of lightening split the sky. Then there was thunder. Beyond the hills, the heavens grew dark.

"Looks like a big rain in the city," said the old man.

"If we had been on time, we'd be sold out by now," grumbled his son.

"Take it easy," said the old gentleman, "you'll last longer."

It wasn't until late in the afternoon that they got to the top of the hill overlooking the town.

They looked down at it for a long time. Neither of them spoke.

Finally the young man who had been in such a hurry said, "I see what you mean, father."

They turned their cart around and drove away from what had once been the city of Hiroshima.

This story is attributed to Billy Rose who included it in one of his "Pitching Horseshoes" columns.

107 YOU'RE NOT LISTENING!

In this riotous energizer partners work hard at "not listening" to each other and the group brainstorms essential components of good listening.

GOALS

To identify key elements of effective listening.

To promote group interaction and playfulness.

GROUP SIZE

Unlimited.

TIME FRAME

5–10 minutes

PROCESS

☞ *This process is an ideal icebreaker for a presentation on listening as a stress management skill. It would fit well with **Stop, Look and Listen**, p 84.*

1) The trainer asks everyone to stand up, mill around the room and grab a partner. When everyone is paired, he announces that this is an exercise in *not listening* and describes the process.

➤ Decide who is *Honolulu* and who is *Fort Lauderdale*.

➤ Partners will take turns. *Fort Lauderdales* will begin by speaking spontaneously on an assigned topic for 30 seconds. While you are speaking, the *Honolulus* should somehow communicate that you are *not* listening to your partners.

☞ *Encourage the "speakers" to put a little punch into their presentation—to speak with energy, passion and pizzazz! Encourage "listeners" to be creative in their non-response.*

2) Once the rules are clear, the trainer gives instructions for the first round.

➤ *Fort Lauderdales*, vividly describe your *favorite ice cream* to your *Honolulu* partner, who will *not listen*. (30–45 seconds)

3) The trainer calls time and asks partners to switch roles.

©1994 Whole Person Press 210 W Michigan Duluth MN 55802   (800) 247-6789

➤ This time the **Honolulus** should describe in detail your *favorite vacation*—real or ideal—while the **Fort Lauderdales** demonstrate *not listening*. (30–45 seconds)

4) Since this *not listening* exercise frustrates direct communication, the trainer offers an opportunity for more satisfying contact between partners.

➤ You now have 10 seconds to make a positive connection with each other in some creative way.

5) After the buzz settles down, participants are invited to pool their knowledge.

➤ Each pair should join another pair. In quartets, spend 2 minutes brainstorming responses to the question:

Based on your recent experience of *not* being listened to, what are the key components of effective listening?

6) The trainer reconvenes the group, solicits examples of good listening components and ties this process into other issues raised in the learning experience.

VARIATIONS

■ Repeat *Steps 2 and 3*, only this time the listeners try to communicate that they *are* listening intently and with understanding. Use new topics such as *favorite restaurant or favorite place in your town*, etc.

■ In *Step 4*, partners brainstorm lists of non-verbal cues that indicate *listening* and those that indicate *not listening*. They then discuss the impact of non-verbals on the communication process and the relationship to stress.

■ In *Step 5*, groups make newsprint posters of *Do's and Don'ts for Listening*. These are posted around the room and used as reminders of listening guidelines in later small group discussions.

Submitted by Joel Goodman.

108 PUSHING MY BUTTONS

In this unusual self-care break participants stimulate several acupressure points to get their energy flowing again.

GOALS

To introduce the concept of energy flow.

To energize and revitalize the group.

TIME FRAME

10–15 minutes

PROCESS

1) The trainer invites participants to join her in a healthy wake-up break based on self-acupressure techniques interpreted from ancient writings found on the walls of the Shaolin Temple in China.

   ➤ You will be massaging specific areas of your body, including many "pressure points," where the body's energy flow can be stimulated.

   ➤ You will discover the exact location of your pressure points by noticing the spots that feel "different" or a little tender. Steady pressure or gentle massage should relieve the pain and release the energy.

2) The trainer suggests that everyone follow along as she talks the group through the 13 steps, describing and demonstrating the various strokes that are used for the different points.

   ☞ *Be sure to experiment with these instructions and find your own pressure points before trying to explain them to the group.*

VARIATION

■ A few of these acupressure points could be introduced at each break. Then toward the end of the learning experience the whole sequence could be done as a unit.

Submitted by Jackie Mosier who learned a process similar to this from her T'ai Chi instructor, Master Marshall Ho.

PUSHING MY BUTTONS:
self-acupressure routine

1) Rub the **top of your head** briskly with both palms.

2) Use both thumbs to locate the depression at **the base of your skull** in back, where it meets the spine. Starting in the middle and moving out toward the sides, staying just below the bony (occipital) ridge, locate pressure points about one inch apart all across the base of the skull.

   Most people have several tender spots in this area, so don't hurry—use enough pressure with your thumbs to **feel** the tenderness at each spot, but not enough pressure to create acute pain. After a few seconds this press can be released or expanded into a gentle circular massage.

3) Rub your **nose** vigorously, kneading, pulling and moving it around. Try a two-handed noserub!

4) Massage the **lobe of each ear** between your thumb and index finger. Make sure the whole perimeter gets a thorough rubdown, then pull gently. Finally, cup your hands over your ears and give the whole area a quick up and down rub.

5) Use your thumbs to trace **along and beneath your lower jaw.** Use moderate pressure and move very slowly. Start in the corners under the ears and follow the jaw bone to the midline, thumbs meeting under your chin.

6) Using the fingers of your right hand, rub **across your chest from the left shoulder to the sternum**, staying below the line of the collarbone. Hold your fingers like a curved garden rake and make strong back-and-forth movements, kneading the muscles as you slowly move across your chest. Repeat on the left side using the right hand.

7) Flex your left arm. Use your right thumb to locate the pressure point **in the crook of your elbow**, just outside the bone of your lower arm. Feel around, using a fair amount of pressure until you find the trigger point. Hold and release. Repeat for the right elbow.

8) Use the thumb and one finger of your right hand to **circle your left wrist**. Hold your hand steady and quickly rotate your left arm in a screwing motion so that the left wrist gets a vigorous massage. Repeat for the right wrist.

9) Make fists with both hands. Now reach back and gently pound the **kidney area** with your fists. At this angle you should get just enough pressure for stimulation.

10) Using both hands in a rhythmic motion, clap and slap both **thighs** up and down and front and back, as far as you can reach and as long as it feels good!

11) Move down to the area of your **kneecap**. Using short back-and-forth strokes with your fingertips, knead the entire area above, around and below the kneecap, extending down to massage the protrusions below and outside of the kneecap. If you find any tender spots, stop, apply more pressure and release.

12) Run your thumb along the **inside of your shin** to a point about 4 fingers above the ankle bone. When you find the tender spot, use a thumb press for several seconds, release and then repeat. Be sure to stimulate the pressure point on both legs.

Pregnant women should **not** stimulate this point.

13) Use whatever strokes feel good and spend as much time as possible **massaging your feet.** Try thumb circles, kneading, pulling, clapping, rubbing—on the top, bottom, sides, edges, between the toes, along the arch, etc. If the room is carpeted, try rubbing the soles of your feet vigorously on the floor.

TRAINER'S NOTES

Resources

GUIDE TO THE RESOURCES SECTION

This resources section is intended to provide assistance for planning and preparation as you develop and expand your stress management training and consulting in various settings.

TIPS FOR TRAINERS p. 136

Imaginative strategies for designing presentations and workshops using the exercises in **Structured Exercises in Stress Management Volume 3** to best advantage.

EDITORS' CHOICE p. 138

Recommendations from the editors on their favorite exercises and teaching designs from this volume that cover job-related stress issues.

Four****Star Exercises: The Best of **Stress 3** p. 138
Especially for the Workplace p. 140

WINNING COMBINATIONS p. 141

Session outlines for using exercises from **Stress 3** in combination to fit different time frames and themes. Plus notes on natural companion processes from other **Structured Exercises** volumes.

Generic Stress Presentation (60–90 min)
Workshop on Stress with Skill-building (Listening/Conflict) (2 hours)
Stress of Change Workshop (90 min–3 hours)

ANNOTATED INDEXES to Stress 3 p. 143

Guides to specific content segments and group activities incorporated in exercises from **Stress 3**, identified by page reference, time frame, brief description and comments on use.

Index to CHALKTALKS p. 143
Index to DEMONSTRATIONS p. 144
Index to PHYSICAL ENERGIZERS p. 145
Index to MENTAL ENERGIZERS p. 146
Index to RELAXATION ROUTINES p. 147

CONTRIBUTORS/EDITORS p. 148

Data on trainers who have shared their best process ideas in this volume. All are highly skilled educators and most provide in-house training, consultation, or workshops that may be valuable to you in planning comprehensive stress management programs. Many contributors are also established authors of well-respected materials on stress, wellness, and training issues.

WHOLE PERSON PUBLICATIONS p. 153

Descriptions of trainer-tested audio, video and print resources available from the stress and wellness specialists.

©1994 Whole Person Press 210 W Michigan Duluth MN 55802   (800) 247-6789

TIPS FOR TRAINERS

Designing Presentations and Workshops Using
Structured Exercises in Stress Management Volume 3

The vast majority of stress management presentations begin with some comprehensive, generic introduction to stress from either the physical or the emotional perspective. Moving from the general to the specific is often an effective way to engage participants, so we have included several exercises in this volume that offer the broad view:

> **79 Spice or Arsenic?** p. 17–20
> **80 Drainers and Energizers** p. 26–29
> **82 Lifetrap 3: Sick of Change** p. 30–39
> **86 S.O.S. for Stress** p. 54–58
> **88 Corporate Presentation** p. 66–67

If, on the other hand, you're interested in trying a really novel approach in your next presentation, why not choose a more specific starting point to "hook" your audience, and then generalize about stress and coping from the data generated by the group? Start by vividly illustrating the stress reaction using one of these effective demonstrations:

> **73B Under Fire** p. 2–3
> **75 Marauders** p. 6–9

Then try one or more of the following exercises as a centerpiece for your workshop. Draw your generalizations from data generated by the group, weaving the participants' insights into your chalktalks and introductions to activities.

● **STRESS focus.** Explore one of three specific sources of stress common to most people: manipulation, role stereotyping or rejection.

> **80 On the Spot** p. 21–25
> **83 Job Descriptions** p. 40–43
> **84 The Last Christmas Tree** p. 44–48

● **COPING focus.** Generate specific stress clusters and plan coping strategies. Or introduce one of two key skills with applications at work and home: conflict management or active listening.

> **87 Stress Clusters Clinic** p. 59–65
> **90 Conflict Management** p. 73–79
> **92 Stop, Look and Listen** p. 84–91

● **RELAXATION focus.** Experiment with one of the three basic forms of relaxation: meditation/guided imagery, autogenic sequences or massage.

> **93 Centering Meditation** p. 92–96

105 Warm Hands p. 125–125
108 Pushing My Buttons p. 131–133

Variety is the spice of life (see exercise 79)! We hope this volume will inspire you to turn on your own creativity and experiment with some fresh approaches to teaching about stress.

©1994 Whole Person Press 210 W Michigan Duluth MN 55802 (800) 247-6789

EDITORS' CHOICE

Although all 36 exercises in this volume are practical, creative and time-tested, we must admit that we use some more often than others. When people call and ask us for suggestions about which exercises to incorporate into their workshop designs, we typically recommend some of our favorites—processes that have worked over and over again with many audiences, readings and activities that are guaranteed to charm a group. We call these our FOUR****STAR choices.

Four****Star Exercises	Page	Comments (Timing)
79 Spice or Arsenic?	p. 17–20	Classic self-assessment from the original **Stress Skills Seminar.** Simple. Clear. Quick. (20–30 min)
81 Drainers and Energizers	p. 26–29	Hopeful exercise for identifying stressors that drain and energizers that refill—at work, at home, at play. Can shorten for use as icebreaker. (10–25 min)
85 Metaphors	p. 49	This right-brain activity helps people develop models for coping using familiar objects as metaphors. (40–50 min)
86 S.O.S. for Stress	p. 54–58	Easy to remember paradigm for group stress management strategies. Application to a personal stressor. (30–50 min)
90 Conflict Management	p. 73–79	Excellent basic presentation of a crucial stress management skill. Easy to expand. (60 min)
93 Centering Meditation	p. 92–96	Don sneaks this powerful meditation into his workshops whenever he can. It always provokes deep feelings and profound insights. (25–40 min)
94 Closing Formation	p. 97–99	Lively ending for a session or workshop. Convert to an icebreaker by recasting questions. (10–30 min)
98 Change Pentagon	p. 110–112	Elegant whole person planning process for managing a stressful situation. (15–30 min)
103 Groans and Moans	p. 120–121	Nancy can pull this off with any group. Don is a bit more shy. We dare you to try this off-beat tension-reliever. (5–10 min)

106 What's the Hurry?   Haunting parable for Type A's.
                       p. 126–128 Unforgettable. (5–10 min)

ESPECIALLY FOR THE WORKPLACE

Workplace Exercise	Page	Comments (Timing)
74 **Agenda Consensus**	p. 4–5	Works well for staff meetings, too. (15 min)
83 **Job Descriptions**	p. 40–43	Examines stress-provoking role stereo-types such as male-female, labor-management, supervisor-supervisee, etc. (60 min)
88 **Corporate Presentation**	p. 66–67	Participants give themselves a lecture about the ten best methods for managing stress. (20–30 min)
90 **Conflict Management**	p. 73–79	Applicable to any work setting. Be sure to customize for your audience. (60 min)
94 **Closing Formation**	p. 97–99	Nice way to spread the insights around the group and provide positive closure. (10–30 min)
97 **My Stress Reduction Program**	p. 107–109	Comprehensive planning process will appeal to straight line thinkers. Build a session around it. (20–30 min)
107 **You're Not Listening**	p. 129–130	Always a hit with work groups. (5–10 min)

©1994 Whole Person Press 210 W Michigan Duluth MN 55802   (800) 247-6789

WINNING COMBINATIONS

Generic Stress Presentation (60–90 min)

Start with the chalktalk and stress thermometer warm-up in Exercise 79, **Spice or Arsenic?**, p. 17 (20–30 min), which helps people focus on their current, past, and target stress level.

Then introduce the overarching paradigm for coping with stress outlined in Exercise 86, **S.O.S. for Stress**, p.54 (30–50 min). As you present the three strategies: Start on the Situation, Start on Self, and Seek out Support, throw in some energizers to illustrate the strategies and give the group a break.

Close your workshop with the powerfully motivating visualization/goal- setting process in Exercise 89, **Imagine Success**, p. 68 (15–30 min).

Workshop on Stress with Skill-Building Component (Listening or Conflict Management) (2 Hours)

When stress management is the topic of a class or workshop, trainers (and participants!) often spend more time on stress than on management. If you'd like to help a group focus on coping, you could build an entire workshop around one of the two major stress management skills appropriate in nearly any setting: listening and managing conflict.

Begin either workshop with Exercise 77, **Traveling Trios**, p. 12 (10–15 min). This lively ice-breaker helps people get acquainted (or re-acquainted) as they compare coping styles. If you'd like a more didactic warm-up, substitute Exercise 86, **S.O.S. for Stress**, p. 54 (30–50 min), which is a good basic introduction to stress management strategies.

- For a **listening skills** focus, introduce the subject with the powerful demonstration, **You're Not Listening**, Exercise 107, p. 129 (5–10 min). Then go on to teach effective listening skills in triads, using Exercise 92, **Stop, Look and Listen**, p. 84 (60 min).

- For a **conflict management** focus, use the thought-provoking demonstration in Exercise 104, **Tug of War**, p. 122 (5–10 min), to help people analyze their typical reactions to conflict. Then teach the four skills for dealing with conflict as presented in Exercise 90, **Conflict Management**, p. 73 (60 min), and allow participants to apply the strategies to specific conflict situations in their lives.

Exercise 95, **Exit Interview**, p. 100 (20–30 min), combines closure with skill practice. Use it with either the **listening** or **conflict** workshop to reinforce the stress management skills that you've presented.

Stress and Change Workshop (90 min–3 hours)

Exercise 82, **Lifetrap 3: Sick of Change**, p. 30 (60–90 min), uses the most famous stress assessment, Holmes and Rahe's **Social Readjustment Rating Scale** as the centerpiece for exploring the role of change in our lives and the stress it creates. All audiences should be able to identify with the issues and appreciate the focus on strategies for managing change. To expand or spice up your presentation, try adding one or more of these "natural companions."

> The stress thermometer in Exercise 79, **Spice or Arsenic?**, p17 (20–30 min), makes a nice additional warm-up to the topic of change.

> Expand **Part B** to include Exercise 87, **Stress Clusters Clinic**, p. 59 (40–60 min). This exercise using PILEUP cards graphically demonstrates the stress of accumulated life changes and the creative options for dealing with it.

> Use the visualization in Exercise 89, **Imagine Success**, p. 68 (15–30 min), to reinforce the planning process, or try Exercise 96, **Recipe for Success with Stress**, p. 104 (25–30 min), after the planning and sharing process. Invite participants to read their recipes out loud.

Don't forget to change the rhythm of your workshop with tension-relieving breaks and creative activities. This volume contains several excellent energizers and demonstrations. Pick one or more that tickle your fancy.

> Sprinkle several energizers from Exercise 91, **Eight-Minute Stress Break**, p. 80 (1 min each), throughout your presentation for a change of pace. Or have some fun as you kick up your heels with Exercise 99, **Kicking Your Stress Can-Can**, p. 113 (5 min).

> Try Exercise 100, **Chinese Swing**, p. 114 (10 min), as a healthy midsession break. This technique practiced regularly can be a powerful antidote to the stress of change. Exercise 101, **Clouds to Sunshine**, p. 116 (3–5 min), teaches a simple yoga stretch as it demonstrates that change is as inevitable as the seasons.

> Creativity, camaraderie, and reinforcement of key concepts are natural outcomes of Exercise 102, **Do-It-Yourself Singalong**, p. 118 (10–15 min), when small groups make up songs about stress and change.

If you have lots of time you might want to add one of these effective warm-ups from other volumes in the series before **Part A**.

> **Life Event Bingo** (**Stress 2**, 10–20 min) was designed specifically to introduce the concepts of Holmes and Rahe's scale while people get acquainted. **Stress Symptom Inventory**, (**Stress 1**, 30–40 min) provides a whole person assessment that really helps people get in touch with the manifestations of stress in their life.

ANNOTATED INDEXES

Index to CHALKTALKS

74 Agenda Consensus   p. 24   Setting an agenda for the learning
                                      experience.

75 Marauders   p. 6, 8 Recognizing the physical stress reaction.

79 Spice or Arsenic?   p. 17   What is the optimal stress level for you?

80 On the Spot   p. 21   Mind control, manipulation and stress.
                              p. 24   Ten Steps to Critical Thinking.

82 Lifetrap 3: Sick of Change   Change can be the spice of life.
                              p. 31   It can also make us sick.
                              p. 32   Change is stressful.
                              p. 33   Stress, change and illness.
                              p. 35   Taking charge of change.

85 Metaphors   p.49   The importance of creativity in stressful
                                      situations; metaphors for managing stress.

86 S.O.S. for Stress   p. 54   Internal and external sources of stress.
                              p. 55   SOS Strategy: Start On the Situation,
                                      Start On Self, Search Out Support.

89 Imagine Success   p. 68   Positive visualization is a powerful stress
                                      management tool.

90 Conflict Management   p. 73   The nature of conflict: stressful and
                                      desirable.
                              p. 75–79 Conflict management strategies: positive
                                      mental attitude, focus on the issue,
                                      increase tolerance, keep it in perspective.

91 Eight-Minute Stress Break   Benefits of stretching and exercising as
                              p. 80   stress management techniques.

92 Stop, Look and Listen   Communication, stress and the coping
                              p. 84   power of listening.
                              p. 85   Elements of empathy: stop, look and
                                      listen!

93 Centering Meditation   p. 92   Relaxation and guided imagery.

103 Moans and Groans   p. 120 Tension-relieving benefits of groaning.

©1994 Whole Person Press 210 W Michigan Duluth MN 55802   (800) 247-6789

Index to DEMONSTRATIONS

73B Under Fire   p. 2   Generates a stress reaction on the spot.
                                      (10–20 min)

75 Marauders   p. 6   This lively circle game graphically
                                      demonstrates the physical symptoms of
                                      stress. (20–30 min)

104 Tug of War   p. 122 Participants pair up to explore alternative
                                      approaches to conflict. (5–10 min)

107 You're Not Listening!   Powerful experience that highlights good
                               p. 129 listening skills by experimenting with
                                      bad ones. (5–10 min)

©1994 Whole Person Press 210 W Michigan Duluth MN 55802   (800) 247-6789

Index to PHYSICAL ENERGIZERS

75 Marauders   p. 6   Powerful *in vivo* demonstration of the
                                   stress reaction. (20–30 min)

77 Traveling Trios   p. 12 Participants move quickly from group to
                                   group describing their coping styles.
                                   (10–15 min)

91 Eight-Minute Stress Break   Nice 15-step stretch routine that can be
                            p. 80 broken up and interspersed throughout a
                                   presentation. (10 min)

94 Closing Formation   p. 97 Round-robin closing reflection with quick-
                                   ly shifting pairs. (10–30 min)

99 Kicking Your Stress   Stress-relieving dance line, accompa-
Can-Can   p. 113 nied by appropriate music. (15 min)

100 Chinese Swing   p. 114 An ancient antidote to stress. (10 min)

101 Clouds to Sunshine p. 116 T'ai Chi exercise. (3–5 min)

108 Pushing My Buttons   Guided self-massage using acupressure
                            p. 131 points. (10–15 min)

Index to MENTAL ENERGIZERS

84 The Last Christmas Tree   Guided fantasy explores the stress of
                              p. 44 rejection. (20–30 min)

85 Metaphors   p. 49 Familiar objects provoke creative ideas
                                     for managing stress. Could be shortened.
                                     (40–50 min)

89 Imagine Success   p. 68 Practice positive visualization as you
                                     imagine yourself successfully using a
                                     specific coping skill. (15–30 min)

93 Centering Meditation   Guided imagery featuring a trip through
                              p. 92 the woods and a conversation with a
                                     wise soul. (25–40 min)

102 Create-A-Singalong   p. 118 Small groups compose stress and coping
                                     lyrics to familiar tunes. (10–15 min)

106 What's the Hurry?   p. 126 Touching parable about the stressful side
                                     effects of striving too hard. (5–10 min)

©1994 Whole Person Press 210 W Michigan Duluth MN 55802   (800) 247-6789

Index to RELAXATION ROUTINES

91 Eight-Minute Stress Break   Systematic routine for energizing that
                          p. 80   can be used daily for stress reduction.
                                  (10 min)

93 Centering Meditation   Meditative guided visualization using the
                          p. 92   **Spiritual Centering** script. (25–40 min)

100 Chinese Swing   p. 114   This combination breathing and move-
                                  ment exercise promotes groundedness
                                  and vitality. (10 min)

101 Clouds to Sunshine   Breathing and stretching while visualizing
                          p. 116   scenes from nature. (3–5 min)

103 Groans and Moans p. 120   An old-fashioned remedy for stress that
                                  really works! (5 min)

105 Warm Hands   p. 124   Classic autogenic relaxation sequence.
                                  (5–10 min)

108 Pushing My Buttons   For relaxation and revitalization, a self-
                          p. 131   care break that stimulates acupressure
                                  points from head to toe. (10–15 min)

©1994 Whole Person Press 210 W Michigan Duluth MN 55802   (800) 247-6789

CONTRIBUTORS

Martha Belknap, MA. 1170 Dixon Road, Gold Hill, Boulder CO 80302. 303/ 447-9642. Marti is an educational consultant with a specialty in creative relaxation and stress management skills. She has 30 years of teaching experience at all levels. Marti offers relaxation workshops and creativity courses through schools, universities, hospitals and businesses. She is the author of **Taming Your Dragons**, a book and cassette tape of creative relaxation activities for home and school.

Jan Berry-Schroeder, MEd. 3122 Park Place, Evanston IL 60201. 708/864-2316. Jan is a consultant, therapist, musician, and writer. She has extensive experience in Employee Assistance Programs and integrating wellness into the workplace. She specializes in bereavement stress management, conflict resolution, women's issues and self-esteem—to all of which she adds fun.

Jim Cathcart, CPAE. PO Box 9075, La Jolla CA 92038. 619/558-8855. Jim is the author of **Relationship Selling** and **Third Thoughts**, as well as an internationally-known speaker and past president of the National Speakers Association.

David G Danskin, PhD. 180 Gray Mountain drive, Sedona AZ 86336. 602/282-2372. David, a professor emeritus of Kansas State University, is the author of **Quicki-Mini Stress-Management Strategies For Work, Home, Leisure** and is co-author with Dorothy V. Danskin of **Quicki-Mini Stress-Management Strategies For You, a Disabled Person**. He is also senior author of **Biofeedback: An Introduction And Guide**. David is now enjoying his retirement in Arizona.

Robert C Fellows, MTS. MindMatters Workshops, PO Box 16557, Minneapolis MN 55416. 612/925-4090. Bob is a widely-respected educator who combines his master's degree in theology from Harvard University with a background as a professional stage mentalist and illusionist. He regularly tours Australia, Canada, and the United States with his captivating presentations on self-responsibility in health. Fellows is the author of **Easily Fooled: New Insights and Techniques for Resting Manipulation**.

Joseph J Giacalone, Program Director, Coors Life Directions Center, Regis University, 3333 Regis Blvd, Denver CO 80221. 303/458-4101. Joe is a health educator and manages a comprehensive health promotion program for students, faculty and staff at a private liberal arts school and also teaches wellness to community college students. He has consulted with businesses and health care providers in developing survival strategies for dealing with the health implications of lifestyle and organizational change.

Jerry Glashagel, Consultant. 1714 N. Hudson, Chicago IL 60614. 312/649-9542. Jerry spent over 20 years with the YMCA in India, New York, Pasadena, Akron and Chicago. He has degrees from the University of Illinois and Yale University, and enjoys facilitating groups, product design, writing and training. He is currently a consultant in Russia, where he is helping small businesses develop.

Joel Goodman, EdD. Director, The HUMOR Project, 110 Spring Street, Saratoga Springs NY 12866. 518/587-8770. Joel is a popular speaker, consultant and seminar leader who has presented to over 500,000 corporate managers, health care leaders, educators, and other helping professionals throughout the U.S. and abroad. Author of 8 books, Joel publishes **Laughing Matters** magazine and HUMOResources mail order bookstore catalog, and sponsors the annual international conference on "The Positive Power of Humor and Creativity."

Pat Miller, 1211 N Basswood Ave, Duluth MN 55811. 218/722-9361. Pat runs her own consulting and teaching business, Pat Miller Training and Development. She teaches workshops, conducts on-sight team building sessions, facilitates retreats, and mediates conflict in the workplace. Her areas of expertise include communication skills, conflict resolution, team development, self-esteem, and stress management.

Jacki Mosier, RN. Certified Family Nurse Practitioner. Acupressurist. 2018 N. Crescent, Flagstaff AZ 86001. 602/774-8845. As a health care professional, Jacki has found a combination of traditional western medical practices, ancient practices involving energy flows and spiritual recognition necessary to achieve good health and wellness.

Louis M Savary, PhD. 3404 Ellenwood Lane, Tampa FL 33618. 813/961-8046. Holder of doctorates in mathematics and spirituality, Louis is co-founder of the Institute for Consciousness and Music, and author of several books including **Sound Health** (with Steven Halpern) and **Passages: A Guide For Pilgrims Of The Mind**.

Marcia A Schnorr, RN EdD. Nursing Instructor, Kishwaukee College, Rt 38 & Malta Rd, Malta IL 60150. 815/825-2086 (w) 815/562-6823 (h). Marcia is the parish nurse of St Paul Lutheran Church, Rochelle IL, 815/562-2744, coordinator of the Lutheran Church-Missouri Synod Parish Nurse Ministry, and an adjunct professor in parish nursing for Concordia University in Wisconsin.

Keith W Sehnert, MD. 4210 Fremont Avenue South, Minneapolis MN 55409. 612/920-0102 (w), 612/824-5134 (h). Keith is a family doctor who has become a leader in the medical self-care movement. He spends much energy in print (**How To Be Your Own Doctor—Sometimes**, **Stress/Unstress** and **Self-care/Wellcare**), and in person, urging people to improve their physical, mental and spiritual well-being. He has an independent practice in St Louis Park MN.

Mary O'Brien Sippel, RN MS. Licensed Psychologist, 22 East St Andrews, Duluth MN 55803. 218/723-6130 (w) 218/724-5935 (h). Educated as a nurse, Mary has spent over 25 years working the field of community health and education. She has conducted seminars on stress management, burnout prevention, and wellness promotion throughout the U.S. She is currently a personal counselor and adjunct faculty member at the College of St Scholastica, Duluth MN. She is also working on **Wildflower Adventures**, a book on getting food and weight in a healthy perspective for children.

Sally Strosahl, MA. Marriage & Family Therapist, 116 S Westlawn, Aurora IL 60506. 708/897-9796. Sally has an MA in clinical psychology; trained at the Wholistic Health Center; researched the relationship between stress and illness. In addition to her private practice in marriage and family therapy, Sally frequently presents workshops in the areas of stress and wellness management, burnout prevention, body image and size acceptance, and marriage enrichment. She particularly enjoys working with "systems" (family, work groups, agencies, business, churches) to help enhance each member's growth and well-being.

Mark Warner, EdD. Assistant Vice president for Human Resources and Facility Management, James Madison University, Harrisonburg VA 22807. 703/568-3685. In addition to his administrative duties, Mark teaches, consults, writes, and presents on the topics of wellness promotion, leadership development, and organizational development.

Randy R Weigel, PhD. Associate Professor, Dept of Home Economics, Univ of Wyoming, Box 3354 Univ Station, Laramie WY 82071. 307/766-5124 (w). Through workshops, study guides and media development, Randy specializes in making stress research understandable and usable by lay audiences. His training in human relations and education allows him to tailor programs to the needs of specific audiences. Randy has trained students, faculty, parents, ranchers, farmers and helping professionals in stress management.

©1994 Whole Person Press 210 W Michigan Duluth MN 55802   (800) 247-6789

FUTURE CONTRIBUTORS

If you have developed an exciting, effective structured exercise you'd like to share with other trainers in the field of stress or wellness, please send it to us for consideration, using the following guidelines:

- Your entry should be written in a format similar to those in this volume.

- Contributors must either guarantee that the materials they submit are not previously copyrighted or provide a copyright release for inclusion in the Whole Person **Structured Exercises** series.

- When you have adapted the work of others, please acknowledge the original source of ideas or activities.

©1994 Whole Person Press 210 W Michigan Duluth MN 55802   (800) 247-6789

EDITORS

All exercises in this volume not specifically attributed to other contributors are the creative efforts of the editors, who have been designing, collecting, and experimenting with structured processes in their teaching, training and consultation work since the late 1960s.

Nancy Loving Tubesing, EdD, holds a masters degree in group counseling and a doctorate in counselor education. She served as editor of the *Society for Wholistic Medicine's* monograph series and articulated the principles of whole person health care in the monograph, **Philosophical Assumptions**. Faculty Associate and Product Development Coordinator at Whole Person Associates, Nancy is always busy compiling and testing teaching designs for future **Structured Exercises** volumes.

Donald A Tubesing, MDiv, PhD, designer of the classic **Stress Skills** seminar and author of the best-selling **Kicking Your Stress Habits**, has been a pioneer in the movement to reintegrate body, mind, and spirit in health care delivery. With his entrepreneurial spirit and background in theology, psychology, and education, Don brings the whole person perspective to his writing, speaking, and consultation in business and industry, government agencies, health care and human service systems.

Nancy and Don have collaborated on many writing projects over the years, beginning with a small-group college orientation project in 1970 and including two self-help books on whole person wellness, **The Caring Question** (Minneapolis: Augsburg, 1983) and **Seeking Your Healthy Balance** (Duluth: Whole Person Press, 1991) and a score of unusual relaxation audiotapes.

The Tubesings have specialized in developing creative stress management programs and packages for client groups such as the national YMCA (8-session course, **The Y's Way to Stress Management**) and Aid Association for Lutherans (**The Stress Kit** multimedia resource for families).

Their most recent efforts have been directed toward combining the process-oriented approach of the **Structured Exercises** series with the power of video. The resulting three six-session interactive video courses, **WellAware, Manage It!**, and **Managing Job Stress**, include participant booklets with worksheets that stimulate personal reflection and application of principles to specific situations, as well as a step-by-step leader manual for guiding group interaction.

©1994 Whole Person Press 210 W Michigan Duluth MN 55802   (800) 247-6789

STRESS AND WELLNESS RESOURCES

STRUCTURED EXERCISES IN STRESS MANAGEMENT, VOLUMES 1ñ5
STRUCTURED EXERCISES IN WELLNESS PROMOTION, VOLUMES 1ñ5
Nancy Loving Tubesing, EdD, Donald A. Tubesing, PhD,
and Sandy Stewart Christian, MSW, Editors

Each book in these two series contains 36 ready-to-use
experiential learning activities, focusing on whole person health
(body, mind, spirit, emotions, relationships, and lifestyle) or
effective stress management.

Developed by an interdisciplinary team of leaders in the
wellness movement nationwide and top stress management professionals, these exercises actively encourage
participants to examine their current attitudes and patterns.
All process designs are clearly explained and have been
thoroughly field-tested with diverse audiences so that
trainers can use them with confidence.

Each volume brims with practical ideas that mix and match, allowing
trainers to develop new programs for varied settings, audiences, and time
frames. Each volume contains **Icebreakers, Action Planners, Closing
Processes,** and **Group Energizers**. The *Wellness Promotion* volumes also
include **Wellness Explorations** and **Self-Care Strategies.** The *Stress
Management* volumes include **Stress Assessments, Management Strategies,** and **Skill Builders.**

  ❑ **Stress or Wellness 8 1/2" x 11" Loose-leaf EditionóVols 1ñ5 / $54.95 each**
  ❑ **Stress or Wellness 6" x 9" Softcover EditionóVols 1ñ5 / $29.95 each**
  ❑ **Worksheet MastersóVols 1ñ5 / $9.95 each**
     ** Worksheet Masters are included as part of the loose-leaf edition.**

STRESS AND WELLNESS REFERENCE GUIDE
**A Comprehensive Index to the Chalktalks, Processes, and Activities in
the Whole Person Structured Exercises Series**
Nancy Loving Tubesing, EdD, Editor

This handy index is your key to over 360 teaching designs in
the ten-volume *Structured Exercises in Stress and Wellness*
seriesóorganized by theme, time frame, level of self-disclo-
sure, trainer experience level, and goals. This book includes all
ten Tips for Trainers sections, with workshop outlines and
suggestions especially for the workplace.

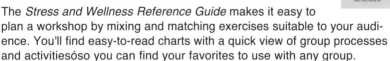

The *Stress and Wellness Reference Guide* makes it easy to
plan a workshop by mixing and matching exercises suitable to your audience. You'll find easy-to-read charts with a quick view of group processes
and activitiesóso you can find your favorites to use with any group.

  ❑ **Stress and Wellness Reference Guide / $29.95**

©1994 Whole Person Press 210 W Michigan Duluth MN 55802   (800) 247-6789

ADDITIONAL GROUP PROCESS RESOURCES

INSTANT ICEBREAKERS
50 Powerful Catalysts for Group Interaction and High-Impact Learning

Sandy Stewart Christian, MSW,
and Nancy Loving Tubesing, EdD, Editors

Introduce the subject at hand and introduce participants to each other with these proven strategies that apply to all kinds of audiences and appeal to many learning styles.

Step-by-step instructions and dazzling graphics on the worksheets make any presentation a breeze.

❑ **Instant Icebreakers / $24.95**
❑ **Worksheet Masters / $9.95**

WORKING WITH WOMENíS GROUPS, Volumes 1 & 2
Louise Yolton Eberhardt

The two volumes of *Working with Women's Groups* have been completely revised and updated. *Volume 1* explores consciousness raising, self-discovery, and assertiveness training. *Volume 2* looks at sexuality issues, women of color, and leadership skills training.

❑ **Working with Womenís Groups, Vols 1 & 2 / $24.95 each**
❑ **Worksheet Masters Vols 1 & 2 / $9.95 each**

WORKING WITH MENíS GROUPS
Roger Karsk and Bill Thomas

Working with Men's Groups has been updated to reflect the reality of menís lives in the 1990s. Each exercise follows a structured pattern to help trainers develop either onetime workshops or ongoing groups that explore menís issues in four key areas: self-discovery, consciousness raising, intimacy, and parenting.

❑ **Working with Menís Groups / $24.95**
❑ **Worksheet Masters / $9.95**

WELLNESS ACTIVITIES FOR YOUTH, Volumes 1 & 2
Sandy Queen

Each volume of *Wellness Activities for Youth* provides 36 complete classroom activities that help leaders teach children and teenagers about wellness with a whole person approach and an emphasis on FUN. The concepts include: values, stress and coping, self-esteem, personal well-being, and social wellness.

❑ **Wellness Activities for Youth, Vols 1 & 2 / $21.95 each**
❑ **Worksheet Masters / $9.95 each**

TOPICAL GROUP RESOURCES

WORKING WITH GROUPS ON SPIRITUAL THEMES
Elaine Hopkins, Zo Woods, Russell Kelley, Katrina Bentley,
and James Murphy

True wellness must address the spirit. Many groups that
originally form around issues such as physical or mental
health, stress management, or relationships eventually
recognize the importance of spiritual issues. The material con-
tained in this manual helps health professionals initiate discussion
on spiritual needs in a logical, organized fashion that induces a
high level of comfort for group members and leaders.

  ❑ **Working with Groups on Spiritual Themes / $24.95**
  ❑ **Worksheet Masters / $9.95**

WORKING WITH GROUPS TO OVERCOME PANIC, ANXIETY, & PHOBIAS
Shirley Babior, LCSW, MFCC, and Carol Goldman, LICSW

Written especially for therapists, this manual presents well-researched, state-
of-the-art treatment strategies for a variety of anxiety disorders. It includes
treatment goals, basic anxiety-recovery exercises, and recovery enhancers
that encourage lifestyle changes. Sessions in this manual are related directly
to the chapters in *Overcoming Panic, Anxiety, & Phobias.*

  ❑ **Working with Groups to Overcome Panic, Anxiety, & Phobias / $24.95**
  ❑ **Worksheet Masters / $9.95**

WORKING WITH GROUPS TO EXPLORE
FOOD & BODY CONNECTIONS
Sandy Stewart Christian, MSW, Editor

This innovative collection of 36 group processes gathered from
experts around the country tackles complex and painful issues
nearly everyone is concerned about́dieting, weight, healthy
eating, fitness, body image, and self-esteeḿusing a whole person
approach that advocates health and fitness for people of all sizes.

  ❑ **Working with Groups to Explore Food & Body Connections / $24.95**
  ❑ **Worksheet Masters / $9.95**

CREATIVE PLANNING FOR THE SECOND HALF OF LIFE
Burton Kreitlow, PhD, and Doris Kreitlow, MS

This is the first book to help group leaders design a presentation or workshop
that addresses the whole-person needs of people ages 50 and up. These 29
structured exercises explore ways of planning for retirement by finding
intriguing ways to make a useful life for yourself́not simply setting aside
money for the day you quit working.

  ❑ **Creative Planning for the Second Half of Life / $24.95**
  ❑ **Worksheet Masters / $9.95**

©1994 Whole Person Press 210 W Michigan Duluth MN 55802   (800) 247-6789

WORKING WITH GROUPS FROM DYSFUNCTIONAL FAMILIES
Cheryl Hetherington

This collection of 29 proven group activities is designed to heal the pain that results from living in a dysfunctional family. With these exercises leaders can promote healing, build self-esteem, encourage sharing, and help participants acknowledge their feelings.

- ❑ Working with Groups from Dysfunctional Families / $24.95
- ❑ Worksheet Masters / $9.95

WORKING WITH GROUPS ON FAMILY ISSUES
Sandy Stewart Christian, MSW, LICSW

These 24 structured exercises combine the knowledge of marriage and family experts with practical techiques to help you move individuals, couples, and families toward positive change. Topics include divorce, single parenting, stepfamilies, gay and lesbian relationhips, working partners, and more.

- ❑ Working with Groups on Family Issues / $24.95
- ❑ Worksheet Masters / $9.95

WORKING WITH GROUPS IN THE WORKPLACE

BRIDGING THE GENDER GAP
Louise Yolton Eberhardt

Bridging the Gender Gap contains a wealth of exercises for trainers to use with men and women who work as colleagues. These activities will also be useful in gender role awareness groups, diversity training, couples workshops, college classes, and youth seminars.

- ❑ Bridging the Gender Gap / $24.95
- ❑ Worksheet Masters / $9.95

CONFRONTING SEXUAL HARASSMENT
Louise Yolton Eberhardt

Confronting Sexual Harassment presents exercises that trainers can safely use with groups to constructively explore the issues of sexual harassment, look at the underlying causes, understand the law, motivate men to become allies, and empower women to speak up.

- ❑ Confronting Sexual Harassment / $24.95
- ❑ Worksheet Masters / $9.95

CELEBRATING DIVERSITY
Cheryl Hetherington

Celebrating Diversity helps people confront and question the beliefs, prejudices, and fears that can separate them from others. Carefully written exercises help trainers present these sensitive issues in the workplace as well as in educational settings.

- ❑ Celebrating Diversity / $24.95
- ❑ Worksheet Masters / $9.95

©1994 Whole Person Press 210 W Michigan Duluth MN 55802   (800) 247-6789

SELF-HELP RESOURCES

OVERCOMING PANIC, ANXIETY, & PHOBIAS
Shirley Babior, LCSW, MFCC, and Carol Goldman, LICSW

This practical self-help guide provides concrete advice as well as hopeful personal stories of recovery. Tips include managing catastrophic thoughts with rational responses, facing fearful situations, dealing with setbacks, and using relaxation to reduce physical symptoms.

❑ **Overcoming Panic, Anxiety, & Phobias / $12.95**

DONíT GET MAD, GET FUNNY!
Leigh Anne Jasheway, Illustrations by Geoffrey Welles

Jasheway guides readers through identifying the seven symptoms of stress, surveying your current stress level, creating a stress management plan, determining the types of things you find humorous, and learning five simple steps to put more humor in your life.

❑ **Donít Get Mad, Get Funny! / $12.95**

SLEEP SECRETS FOR SHIFT WORKERS & PEOPLE WITH OFF-BEAT SCHEDULES
David Morgan

Twenty-five million people in the United States work shifts, and half of them report sleep problems. *Sleep Secrets*óthe first book to address the unique problems shift workers faceóhelps people improve the quality of their sleep so they can lead happier, healthier, more prodcutive lives.

❑ **Sleep Secrets / $12.95**

WORKSHOPS-IN-A-BOOK

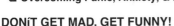

KICKING YOUR STRESS HABITS
A Do-It-Yourself Guide for Coping with Stress
Donald A. Tubesing, PhD

This workshop-in-a-book actively involves the reader in assessing stressful patterns and developing more effective coping strategies. The 10-step planning process and 20 skills for managing stress make *Kicking Your Stress Habits* an ideal text for stress management classes in many different settings, from hospitals to universities.

❑ **Kicking Your Stress Habits / $15.95**

SEEKING YOUR HEALTHY BALANCE
A Do-It-Yourself Guide to Whole Person Well-Being
Donald A. Tubesing, PhD, and Nancy Loving Tubesing, EdD

Seeking Your Healthy Balance helps readers discover how to develop a more balanced lifestyle by learning effective ways to juggle work, self, and others; by clarifying self-care options; and by discovering and setting their own personal priorities.

❑ **Seeking Your Healthy Balance / $15.95**

©1994 Whole Person Press 210 W Michigan Duluth MN 55802   (800) 247-6789

RELAXATION AUDIOTAPES

SENSATIONAL RELAXATIONó$11.95 each
When stress piles up, it becomes a heavy load both
physically and emotionally. These full-length relaxation
experiences will teach you techniques that can be used
whenever you feel that stress is getting out of control.
Choose one you like and repeat it daily until it becomes second nature, then
recall that technique whenever you need it or try a new one every day.

- **Countdown to Relaxation** / Countdown 19:00, Staircase 19:00
- ❑ **Daybreak / Sundown** / Daybreak 22:00, Sundown 22:00
- **Take a Deep Breath** / Breathing for Relaxation 17:00, Magic Ball 17:00
- ❑ **Relax . . . Let Go . . . Relax** / Revitalization 27:00, Relaxation 28:00
- **StressRelease** / Quick Tension Relievers 22:00, Progressive Relaxation 20:00
- ❑ **Warm and Heavy** / Warm 24:00, Heavy 23:00

STRESS BREAKSó$11.95 each
Do you need a short energy booster or a quick stress reliever? If you donít
know what type of relaxation you like, or if you are new to guided relaxation
techniques, try one of our **Stress Breaks** for a quick refocusing or change of
pace any time of the day.

- ❑ **BreakTime** / Solar Power 8:00, Belly Breathing 9:00, Fortune Cookie 9:00,
  Mother Earth 11:00, Big Yawn 5:00, Affirmation 11:00
- ❑ **Natural Tranquilizers** / Clear the Deck 10:00, Body Scan 10:00,
  99 Countdown 10:00, Calm Down 9:00, Soothing Colors 11:00, Breathe Ten 9:00
- ❑ **Stress Escapes** / Sensory Relaxation 18:00, Breathing Meditation 11:00,
  Anchoring 12:00, Breathe Away Tension 8:00, Moans and Groans 9:00
- ❑ **Worry Stoppers** / 10-Second Breathing 5:00, Trouble Bubbles 5:45, Train of
  Thought 5:30, Rest in Peace 6:00, Passive Progressive Relaxation 22:00

DO-IT-YOURSELF RELAXATIONó$11.95 each
Learn the basics of specialized techniques you can use whenever you need
them to trigger your bodyís relaxation response.

- ❑ **Yoga** / Cleansing Breath 6:30, Good Morning World 11:00, Relaxation Pose 10:30,
  Complete and Humming Breath 9:00, Cobra 10:00, Seaweed and Oak 9:00
- ❑ **Massage** / Pushing My Buttons 18:00, All Ears 5:00, Fingertip Face Massage
  15:00, Eye Soothers 7:00

DAYDREAMSó$11.95 each
Escape from the stress around you with guided tours to beautiful places. The
quick escapes in our **Daydreams** tapes will lead your imagination away from
your everyday cares so you can resume your tasks relaxed and comforted.

- ❑ **Daydreams 1: Getaways** / Cabin Retreat 11:00, Night Sky 10:00, Hot Spring
  7:00, Mountain View 8:00, Superior Sail 8:00
- ❑ **Daydreams 2: Peaceful Places** / Ocean Tides 11:00, City Park 10:00,
  Hammock 8:00, Meadow 11:00
- ❑ **Daydreams 3: Relaxing Retreats** / Melting Candle 5:00, Tropical Paradise
  10:00, Sanctuary 7:00, Floating Clouds 5:00, Seasons 9:00, Beach Tides 9:00

GUIDED MEDITATIONó$11.95 each
Take a step beyond relaxation. The imagery in our full-length meditations will help you discover your strengths, find healing, make positive life changes, and recognize your inner wisdom.

- ❏ **Inner Healing /** Inner Healing 20:00, Peace with Pain 20:00
- ❏ **Personal Empowering /** My Gifts 22:00, Hidden Strengths 21:00
- ❏ **Healthy Balancing /** Inner Harmony 20:00, Regaining Equilibrium 20:00
- ❏ **Spiritual Centering /** Spiritual Centering 20:00 (male and female narration)
- ❏ **Mantras /** Illumination 23:00, Transformation 23:00

WILDERNESS DAYDREAMSó$11.95 each
Discover the healing power of nature with the four tapes in our **Wilderness Daydreams** series. The eight special journeys will transport you from your harried, stressful surroundings to the peaceful serenity of words and water.

- ❏ **Canoe / Rain /** Canoe 19:00, Rain 22:00
- ❏ **Island / Spring /** Island 19:00, Spring 19:00
- ❏ **Campfire / Stream /** Campfire 17:00, Stream 19:00
- ❏ **Sailboat / Pond /** Sailboat 25:00, Pond 25:00

MINI-MEDITATIONSó$11.95 each
These brief guided visualizations begin by focusing your breathing and uncluttering your mind so that you can concentrate on a sequence of sensory images that promote relaxation, centering, healing, growth, and spiritual awareness.

- ❏ **Healing Visions /** Rocking Chair 5:00, Pine Forest 8:00, Long Lost Confidant 10:00, Caterpillar to Butterfly 7:00, Superpowers 9:00, Tornado 8:00
- ❏ **Refreshing Journeys /** 1 to 10 10:00, Thoughts Library 11:00, Visualizing Change 6:00, Magic Carpet 9:00, Pond of Love 9:00, Cruise 9:00
- ❏ **Healthy Choices /** Lifestyle 7:15, Eating 7:30, Exercise 7:15, Stress 7:30, Relationships 7:00, Change 7:30

DO-IT-YOURSELF WELLNESS
Make mind/body self-care breaks an integral part of your wellness lifestyle with these affirming breathing and imagery routines for special needs.

- ❏ **Eating /** Mealtime Meditation 13:00, Filling Your Empty Spaces 15:00, Mood Surfing 11:00, Hungers 17:00
- ❏ **Body Image /** Relaxing Breath 5:45, Body Sensing 14:15, Body Talk 12:00, Cleansing Breath Relaxation 5:45, Eyes of Love 26:15
- ❏ **Calm Down /** Progressive Relaxation 25:00, Calming BreathóPeaceful Pool 14:00, Mindful Meditation 11:00

MUSIC ONLYó$11.95 each
No relaxation program would be complete without relaxing melodies to play as background for a prepared script or to enjoy favorite techniques on your own. Steven Eckels composed his melodies specifically for relaxation. These ìmusical prayers for healingî will calm your body, mind, and spirit.

- ❏ **Tranquility /** Awakening 20:00, Repose 20:00
- ❏ **Harmony /** Waves of Light 30:00, Rising Mist 10:00, Frankincense 10:00, Angelica 10:00
- ❏ **Serenity /** Radiance 20:00, Quiescence 10:00, Evanescence 10:00

MUSIC ONLY CDó$15.95
- ❏ **Contemplation /** Mystical Meditation 31:00, Musical Mantras 31:00

ADDITIONAL TRAINERS RESOURCES

PLAYFUL ACTIVITIES FOR POWERFUL PRESENTATIONS
Bruce Williamson

Spice up presentations with healthy laughter. The 40 creative energizers in *Playful Activities for Powerful Presentations* will enhance learning, stimulate communication, promote teamwork, and reduce resistance to group interaction.

❑ **Playful Activities for Powerful Presentations / $21.95**

MIND-BODY MAGIC
Martha Belknap, MA

Make any presentation more powerful with one of these 40 feel-good activities. Handy tips with each activity show you how to use it in your presentation, plus ideas for enhancing or extending the activity, and suggestions for adapting it for your teaching goals and audience. Use *Mind-Body Magic* to present any topic with pizzazz!

❑ **Mind-Body Magic / $24.95**
❑ **Worksheet Masters/ $9.95**

CREATING A CLIMATE FOR POWER LEARNING
37 Mind-Stretching Activities
Carolyn Chambers Clark, EdD, ARNP

Creative warmup processes that prepare leaders and participants for a satisfying learning experience. These activities will enhance your presentation skills, leadership style, and teaching effectiveness no matter what your audience or setting.

❑ **Creating a Climate for Power Learning / $21.95**

ACTING OUT
Improvisational Tools for Teaching
Izzy Gesell, MS

Novice-friendly improvisational theater techniques adapted for community or workplace groups focused on personal development or organizational change. Use these intriguing tools in presentations, workshops, or classes to build self-esteem, encourage creative thinking, promote team building, and support problem solving.

❑ **Acting Out / $21.95**

To order, call toll free (800) 247-6789
or visit our website at
http://www.wholeperson.com/wpa

©1994 Whole Person Press 210 W Michigan Duluth MN 55802   (800) 247-6789

MIND-BODY WELLNESS

Annotated resource guide to books, journals, audio and videotapes, publications, organizations, catalogs, information sources, self-help groups, teaching tools for whole-person well-being
Jim Polidora, PhD

Locate hard-to-find information quickly and easliy with this comprehensive bibliography and mind-body wellness Yellow Pages. *Mind-Body Wellness* lists over 2,000 of the best classical and contemporary resources drawn from the fields of health and wellness, physical education, human services, psychology, education, psychiatry, and alternative approaches to well-being.

❑ **Mind-Body Wellness / $29.95**

RELAXATION RESOURCES

30 SCRIPTS FOR RELAXATION, IMAGERY, & INNER HEALING, VOLUMES 1 & 2
Julie Lusk

The relaxation scripts, creative visualizations, and guided meditations in these volumes were created by experts in the field of guided imagery. Both volumes include information on how to use the scripts, suggestions for tailoring them to specific needs and audiences, and information on how to successfully incorporate guided imagery into existing programs. *Volume 1* available in Spanish.

❑ **30 Scripts for Relaxation, Imagery, & Inner Healing Vols 1 & 2 / $21.95 each**

INQUIRE WITHIN
Andrew Schwartz

Use visualization to help people make positive changes in their lives. The 24 visualization experiences in *Inquire Within* will help participants enhance their creativity, heal inner pain, learn to relax, and deal with conflict. Each visualization includes questions at the end of the process that encourage deeper reflection and a better understanding of the exercise and the response it evokes.

❑ **Inquire Within / $21.95**

GUIDED IMAGERY FOR GROUPS
Andrew Schwartz

Ideal for courses, workshops, team-building, and personal stress management, this comprehensive resource includes scripts for 50 thematic visualizations that promote calming, centering, creativity, congruence, clarity, coping, and connectedness. Detailed instructions for using relaxation techniques and guided images in group settings allow educators at all levels, in any setting, to help people tap into the healing and creative powers of imagery.

❑ **Guided Imagery for Groups / $24.95**

WHOLE PERSON PRODUCTS

Stress and Wellness Series
* Structured Exercises in Stress Management Volumes 1ñ5 (softcover) .. each $29.95
  Structured Exercises in Stress Management Volumes 1ñ5 (loose-leaf) . each $54.95
* Structured Exercises in Wellness Promotion Volumes 1ñ5 (softcover) .. each $29.95
  Structured Exercises in Wellness Promotion Volumes 1ñ5 (loose-leaf) . each $54.95
  Stress & Wellness Reference Guide (index to series) $29.95

Tools for Working with Groups
* Working with Womenís Groups, Volumes 1 & 2...................................... each $24.95
* Working with Menís Groups $24.95
* Working with Groups from Dysfunctional Families.. $24.95
* Working with Groups on Spiritual Themes $24.95
* Celebrating Diversity $24.95
* Bridging the Gender Gap $24.95
* Confronting Sexual Harassment $24.95
* Working with Groups to Explore Food & Body Connections $24.95
* Working with Groups to Overcome Panic, Anxiety, & Phobias $24.95
* Working with Groups to Explore Family Issues... $24.95
* Working with Groups: Creative Planning for the Second Half of Life $24.95

Working with Young People
* Wellness Activities for Youth, Volumes 1 & 2... each $21.95
  What Do You Do with a Child Like This?.. $15.95

* Companion Worksheet Masters are available for all books marked with a *
  Worksheet Masters... each volume $9.95

Trainers Resources
  Playful Activities for Powerful Presentations $21.95
  30 Scripts for Relaxation, Imagery, & Inner Healing, Volumes 1 & 2 ...... each $21.95
  Inquire Within (imagery / meditation) $21.95
  Guided Imagery for Groups.. $24.95
  Mind-Body Wellness: An Annotated Bibliography $29.95
  Mind-Body Magic $21.95
  Creating a Climate for Power Learning $21.95
  Acting Out: Improvisational Tools for Teaching $21.95

Self-Help Books
  Kicking Your Stress Habits $15.95
  Seeking Your Healthy Balance $15.95
  Overcoming Panic, Anxiety, & Phobias $12.95
  Sleep Secrets $12.95
  Donít Get Mad, Get Funny! $12.95

Video Resources
  Making Healthy Choices Series (6 videos, Leader & Skill Building Guides) $475.00
  Single session videos available (each tape includes 5 guides) .... each $95.00
    Session 1: Healthy Lifestyle / Session 2: Healthy Eating / Session 3:
    Healthy Exercise / Session 4: Healthy Stress / Session 5: Healthy
    Relationships / Session 6: Healthy Change

  Managing Job Stress Series (6 videos, Leader & Skill Building Guides) $475.00
  Single session videos available (each tape includes 5 guides) .... each $95.00
    Session 1: Handling Workplace Pressure / Session 2: Clarifying Roles
    and Expectations / Session 3: Controlling the Workload / Session 4:
    Managing People Pressures / Session 5: Surviving the Changing
    Workplace / Session 6: Balancing Work and Home

Manage It! Series (6 videos, Leader & Skill Building Guides) $475.00
    Single session videos available (each tape includes 5 guides) .... each $95.00
        Session 1: Stress Traps / Session 2: Stress Overload / Session 3:
        Interpersonal Conflict / Session 4: Addictive Patterns / Session 5: Job
        Stress / Session 6: Survival Skills

Team Esteem Series (6 videos, Leader & Skill Building Guides) $475.00
    Single session videos available (each tape includes 5 guides) .... each $95.00
        Session 1: Overview: The Team Esteem Difference / Session 2: Team
        Talk / Session 3: Team Energy / Session 4: Team Artistry / Session 5:
        Team Mission / Session 6: Putting Team Esteem to Work

Audio Resources
Stress Breaks
    BreakTime $11.95
    Natural Tranquilizers $11.95
    Stress Escapes $11.95
    Worry Stoppers $11.95
Daydreams
    Daydreams 1: Getaways $11.95
    Daydreams 2: Peaceful Places $11.95
    Daydreams 3: Relaxing Retreats $11.95
Wilderness Daydreams
    Canoe / Rain $11.95
    Island / Spring $11.95
    Campfire / Stream $11.95
    Sailboat / Pond $11.95
Sensational Relaxation
    Countdown to Relaxation $11.95
    Daybreak / Sundown $11.95
    Take a Deep Breath $11.95
    Relax . . . Let Go . . . Relax $11.95
    Stress Release $11.95
    Warm & Heavy $11.95
Mini Meditations
    Healing Visions $11.95
    Refreshing Journeys $11.95
    Healthy Choices $11.95
Guided Meditation
    Inner Healing $11.95
    Personal Empowering $11.95
    Healthy Balancing $11.95
    Spiritual Centering $11.95
    Mantras $11.95
Do-It-Yourself Relaxation
    Yoga $11.95
    Massage $11.95
Do-It-Yourself Wellness
    Eating $11.95
    Body Image $11.95
    Calm Down $11.95
Relaxation / Meditation Music
    Tranquility $11.95
    Harmony $11.95
    Serenity $11.95
    Contemplation (CD) $15.95

ABOUT WHOLE PERSON ASSOCIATES

At Whole Person Associates weíre 100% committed to providing stress and wellness materials that involve participants and provide a ìwhole personî focusóbody, mind, spirit, and relationships.

ABOUT THE OWNERS

Whole Person Associates was created by the vision of two people: Donald A. Tubesing, PhD, and Nancy Loving Tubesing, EdD. Don and Nancy have been active in the stress management/wellness promotion movement for over twenty yearsóconsulting, leading seminars, writing, and publishing. Most of our early products were the result of their creativity and expertise. Living proof that you can ìstay evergreen,î Don and Nancy remain the driving force behind the company and are still very active in developing new products that touch peopleís lives.

ABOUT THE COMPANY

Whole Person Associates was ìbornî in Duluth, Minnesota, and we remain committed to our lovely city on the shore of Lake Superior. We put the same high quality into every product we offer, translating the best of current research into practical, accessible, easy-to-use materials. We create the best possible resources to help our customers teach about stress management and wellness promotion. And our friendly, resourceful employees are committed to helping you find the products that fit your needs.

We also strive to treat our customers as we would like to be treated. If we fall short of our goals in any way, please let us know.

ABOUT OUR ASSOCIATES

Who are the ìassociatesî in Whole Person Associates? Theyíre the trainers, authors, musicians, and others who have developed much of the material you see on these pages. Weíre always on the lookout for high-quality products that reflect our ìwhole personî philosophy and fill a need for our customers. Our products were developed by experts who are at the top of their fields, and weíre very proud to be associated with them.

ABOUT OUR CUSTOMERS

Weíd love to hear from you! Let us know what you think of our productsó how you use them in your work, what additional products youíd like to see, and what shortcomings youíve noted. Write us or call on our toll-free line. We look forward to hearing from you!

Call 1-800-247-6789 to receive a catalog or to place an order